bags
PILLOWS
& pincushions

For general information about our other products and services,
please contact our Customer Care Department within the United States
at (800) 762-2974, outside the United States at (317) 572-3993 or fax
(317) 572-4002.

Wiley also publishes its books in a variety of electronic formats.
Some content that appears in print may not be available in electronic
books. For more information about Wiley products, visit our web site
at www.wiley.com.

ISBN 978-0-470-88707-3

Printed in the United States of America

10 9 8 7 6 5 4 3 2

Better Homes and Gardens®

bags PILLOWS & pincushions

Favorites from the Editors of
AMERICAN PATCHWORK & QUILTING®

WILEY

John Wiley & Sons, Inc.

54

60

76

83

134

148

contents

bags

pillows

welcome!

If you're the type of person who loves to create—whether it's the perfect bag to carry to the farmer's market, a standout toss pillow for a chair, or a one-of-a-kind pincushion for a sewing friend—this book will inspire you with page after page of beautiful accessories.

Overflowing with over 35 projects, this beginner-friendly collection is filled with must-have accessories for using up scraps or for showcasing beautiful fabrics. There are so many projects to choose from, the hardest part of the process is deciding which project to make first. Enjoy!

pincushions

back to basics

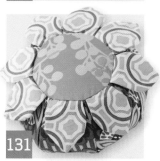

bags

Whether you need to stow a little or a lot, here you'll find the perfect tote, purse, or clutch to carry all your essentials in style. Make several in your favorite fabrics and you'll always have a coordinating bag to match your outfit.

The secret to this striking but simple bag is the fabric choice—an eye-popping print for the body complements a colorful small-scale print for the border.

hold-everything bag

DESIGNER **JEAN BAILEY**
PHOTOGRAPHERS **KRITSADA AND GREG SCHEIDEMANN**

materials

- ⅝ yard green floral (bag body, straps)
- ¼ yard pink-and-green geometric print (bag band)
- ¾ yard circle print (lining, strap lining, pocket)
- 1¼ yards of 22"-wide heavyweight fusible interfacing

Finished tote bag: 10×15×5"

Quantities are for 44/45"-wide, 100% cotton fabrics.
Measurements include ¼" seam allowances. Sew with right sides together unless otherwise stated.

Enjoy the roomy interior of this basic tote. A small interior pocket keeps cell phones, keys, and other small items accessible.

cut fabrics

Cut pieces in the following order.

From green floral, cut:
- 2—1¾×22" strips
- 2—14×15½" rectangles

From pink-and-green geometric print, cut:
- 2—4½×15½" rectangles

From circle print, cut:
- 2—1¾×22" strips
- 2—15½×18" rectangles
- 1—6×9½" rectangle

From interfacing, cut:
- 2—1¼×22" strips
- 2—14×15½" rectangles
- 2—4½×15½" rectangles

assemble bag body and straps

1. Fuse an interfacing 14×15½" rectangle to wrong side of each green floral 14×15½" rectangle. Then fuse an interfacing 4½×15½" rectangle to wrong side of each pink-and-green geometric print 4½×15½" rectangle.

2. Referring to **Diagram 1**, sew together a fused green floral rectangle and a fused geometric print rectangle; press seam toward geometric print rectangle. Topstitch ⅛" above seam line to make bag front. Repeat to make a matching bag back.

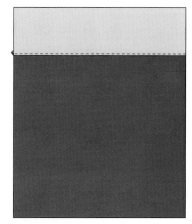

DIAGRAM 1

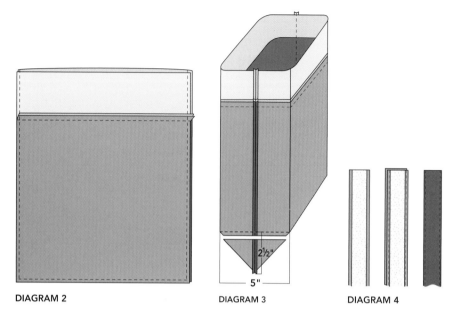

DIAGRAM 2

DIAGRAM 3

2½"

5"

DIAGRAM 4

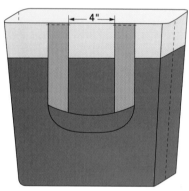

4"

DIAGRAM 5

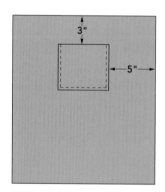

3"

5"

DIAGRAM 6

3. Layer bag front and back; sew together side and bottom edges (**Diagram 2**). Using tip of iron, carefully press seam open.

4. To shape a flat bottom for bag, at one corner match bottom seam line to side seam line, creating a flattened triangle (**Diagram 3**). Measure and mark on seam allowance 2½" from point of triangle. Draw a 5"-long line across triangle, and sew on drawn line. Trim excess fabric. Repeat at remaining bottom corner to make bag body. Turn bag body right side out.

5. Center an interfacing 1¼×22" strip on wrong side of a green floral 1¾×22" strip; fuse. Layer fused green floral strip with a circle print 1¾×22" strip (**Diagram 4**). Stitch together strips' long edges; avoid catching interfacing in seams. Turn right side out and press flat; topstitch ⅛" from long edges to make a strap. Repeat to make a second strap.

6. Referring to **Diagram 5**, pin a strap's raw ends to front edge of bag body; make sure strap is centered with 4" between the ends. Baste strap ends to bag body a scant ¼" from bag's edge. Repeat with second strap and bag back.

assemble pocket and lining

1. Fold circle print 6×9½" rectangle in half with right side inside to form a 6×4¾" rectangle. Sew along the three open edges, leaving a 3" opening in long edge, to make a pocket. Turn pocket right side out through opening and press flat, turning under raw edges at opening.

editor's tip

Timtex, a stiff interfacing popular for making fabric bowls, makes a great removable stabilizer for the bag bottom.

Cut a 5×10" rectangle of Timtex and use fusible web to fuse a 6×11" fabric rectangle to each side. Let cool, then trim the fabric edges close to the Timtex.

2. Referring to **Diagram 6** for placement, position pocket on right side of one circle print 15½×18" rectangle; pin in place. Edgestitch pocket to circle print rectangle along pocket's side and bottom edges; leave top edge open.

3. Layer two circle print 15½×18" rectangles; sew together side and bottom edges, leaving a 6" opening along bottom edge for turning bag right side out. Using tip of iron, carefully press seams open to make bag lining.

4. Shape a flat bottom for lining as in Assemble Bag Body and Straps, Step 4. Leave lining wrong side out.

assemble tote bag

1. Insert bag body inside bag lining with right sides together; straps should be between bag and lining. Align raw edges and seams. Stitch together upper edges of bag body and lining, backstitching over each strap for reinforcement.

2. Turn bag and lining right side out through opening in lining; then pull lining out of bag. Machine-stitch opening of lining closed.

3. Insert lining back into bag and press upper edge. Topstitch ⅛" from upper edge to complete tote bag.

details, details

Personalize your bag simply by using your favorite print. Or add appliqués, trim, or other details for more drama.

Print a photo or other design on an ink-jet fabric sheet; then machine-blanket-stitch it to the front of the bag.

Embellish a silk douppioni bag with folded strips of cotton, raw silk, and faux suede layered and sewn to the bag's upper edge before adding faux-leather band.

Add beaded trim; if the trim header is decorative, hand-sew it over the bag/band seam. If it's not, baste the header to the bag's upper edge and attach the band.

Pair a novelty print or solid with popular stripe fabric for fun combinations that are in style.

in the BAG

Construct this simple over-the-shoulder bag in no time using an inside-out sandwich technique. You'll want to make one for yourself and more for gifts.

DESIGNER **WEEKS RINGLE AND BILL KERR**
PHOTOGRAPHER **GREG SCHEIDEMANN**

materials

- ½ yard red-and-black print (body)
- ½ yard solid black (lining)
- 1¾ yards of 2"-wide black webbing (straps)
- ⅝ yard low-loft polyester batting
- Black ponytail band
- 1"-diameter toggle button
- Jeans needle

Finished backpack: 12×13×1½"

Quantities are for 44/45"-wide, 100% cotton fabrics.
Measurements include ¼" seam allowances. Sew with right sides together unless otherwise stated.

cut fabrics

Cut pieces in the following order.

From red-and-black print, cut:
- 1—15½×36½" rectangle

From solid black, cut:
- 1—15½×36½" rectangle

From black webbing, cut:
- 2—30"-long strips

From polyester batting, cut:
- 1—15½×36½" rectangle
- 2—2×30" strips

attach button loop

1. Form black ponytail band into a figure-eight shape, then place the center of the band along one short edge of red-and-black print 15½×36½" rectangle; sew in place (**Diagram 1**). Trim top of ponytail band off above stitching.

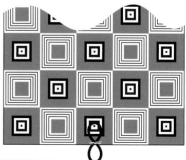

DIAGRAM 1

DIAGRAM 2

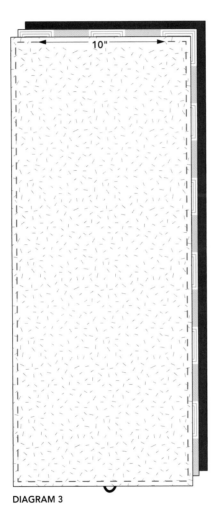

10"

DIAGRAM 3

quilt patchwork panel

1. Lay solid black 15½×36½" rectangle right side up on a flat surface. Aligning edges, place red-and-black print 15½×36½" rectangle, right side down, atop black rectangle (**Diagram 2**). Layer batting on top of red-and-black print rectangle.

2. Mark a 10" opening along the short edge opposite the button loop edge (**Diagram 3**.) Begin at the marked 10" opening and sew together all sides ending at the opposite end of the marked opening. Trim batting from seam allowances to reduce bulk.

3. Turn right side out through opening, pin or baste along sewn edges, and press. Fold opening seam allowances to inside and topstitch to make layered patchwork panel. Press.

4. Quilt as desired.

finish backpack

1. Align one end of each strap on patchwork panel, centered and approximately 12" up from button loop. Stitch securely in place, using a jeans needle (**Diagram 4**).

2. Right sides together, fold bottom of quilted panel up 13½". Pin side edges. Insert free ends of straps through side edges (**Diagram 5**). Pin and check fit, adjusting length of straps if needed. Sew side edges of bag, securing straps in place.

3. To shape flat bottom of bag, at one corner match center bottom of bag to side seam line, creating a flattened triangle (**Diagram 6**). Measuring ¾" from point of triangle, draw a 1½"-long line across triangle. Sew on drawn line. Repeat with remaining bottom corner. Turn bag body right side out.

4. Fold flap over bag front. Sew button to bag front, opposite the button loop on flap, to complete the backpack.

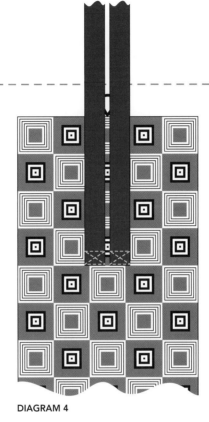

DIAGRAM 4

DIAGRAM 5

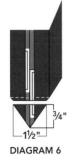

DIAGRAM 6

One bag is not enough! This smart bag has a removable contents pouch that makes changing bags a breeze.

quick-change
purse

DESIGNER **MISSIE CARPENTER**
PHOTOGRAPHER **GREG SCHEIDEMANN**

materials

- ½ yard green print (bag)
- 6×24" piece stable synthetic leather (bag sides, strap)
- ⅓ yard light green print (lining)
- ⅓ yard fusible interfacing
- ⅓ yard clear, heavyweight vinyl (liner)
- 2 brad rings
- Magnetic snap closure
- Polyester thread

Finished Bag: 7½×11×4¼".

Quantities are for 44/45"-wide, 100% cotton fabrics unless otherwise indicated.
Measurements include ¼" seam allowances. Sew with right sides together unless otherwise stated.

This simple-shape bag is trimmed with synthetic leather (you may know it as "pleather") and closed with a clever magnetic snap. With its easy-to-make design, you'll be inspired to whip up an armload in a variety of fabrics. And the secret for a quick change? A clear vinyl contents pouch that easily slips into the bag.

cut fabrics

Cut pieces in the following order.

From green print, cut:
- 2—10½×13½" rectangles
- 2—2"-diameter circles

From synthetic leather, cut:
- 1—2½×24" strip (or desired length for strap)
- 2—1½×20½" strips

From light green print, cut:
- 2—10½×15½" lining rectangles

From fusible interfacing, cut:
- 2—10½×15½" rectangles

From clear, heavyweight vinyl, cut:
- 2—10×16" rectangles

assemble bag

1. Sew together long edges of green print rectangles to make 13½×20½" bag rectangle. Press seam open.

2. Join synthetic leather 1½×20½" strips to opposite edges of bag rectangle. Finger-press each seam toward fabric center; topstitch ⅛" from seam (**Diagram 1**).

DIAGRAM 1

DIAGRAM 2

2⅛"

4¼"

DIAGRAM 3

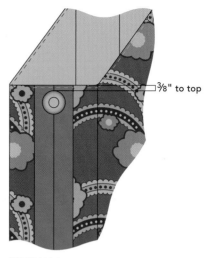

⅜" to top

DIAGRAM 4

3. Fold bag rectangle in half on seam line; sew together side edges (**Diagram 2**). Finger-press seams open.

4. To shape flat bottom for bag, at one corner match bottom seam line to side seam line, creating a flattened triangle (**Diagram 3**). Measuring 2⅛" from point of triangle, draw a 4¼"-long line across triangle. Sew on drawn line. Trim excess fabric. Repeat with remaining bottom corner to make bag body. Turn bag body right side out and finger-press.

5. Following manufacturer's instructions, fuse 10½×15½" interfacing rectangle to wrong side of each light green print 10½×15½" lining rectangle. The interfacing gives the fabric more body and helps the bag retain its shape.

6. Repeat Step 1 with lining rectangles, leaving a 4" opening in seam, to make a 15½×20½" pieced lining rectangle. Press seam open.

7. Repeat Step 3 with pieced lining rectangle.

8. Repeat Step 4 to shape bottom corners of lining. Do not turn lining right side out.

9. Insert bag body into lining, right sides together. Sew together around top edge.

10. Turn bag body and lining to right side through opening in lining bottom seam. Topstitch opening closed. Push lining down into bag body and press upper edge of bag from lining side, taking care to avoid synthetic leather. Topstitch ³⁄₁₆" from upper edge through all layers.

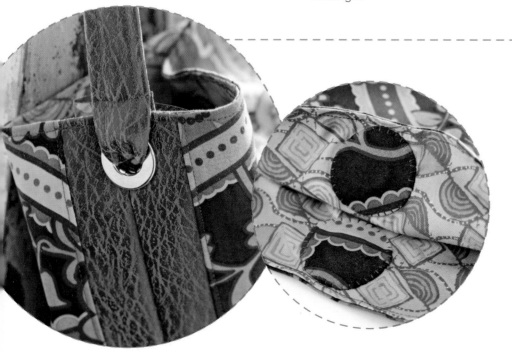

editor's tip

To sew on synthetic leather or vinyl, use a 140/16 HJ needle, polyester thread, a long stitch (3.5 mm), and a Teflon or roller foot. Rather than pins, hold layers together with paper clips to prevent making permanent holes.

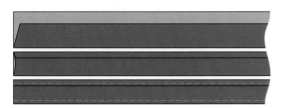

DIAGRAM 5

DIAGRAM 6

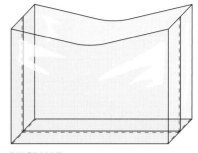

DIAGRAM 7

add strap

1. Center brad ring on bag synthetic leather strip, ⅜" from bag top edge (**Diagram 4**). Trace inner hole of ring on synthetic leather strip. Cut away marked hole, cutting through synthetic leather and lining at same time. (Missie suggests using a seam ripper to make a small cut through all layers to start hole.) Following manufacturer's directions, secure a brad ring to side edge of bag. Repeat to secure ring to opposite side edge.

2. Finger-press under 1", wrong side inside, along one long edge of synthetic leather 2½×24" strip (**Diagram 5**). Finger-press under ½" along remaining long edge. Topstitch ¼" from folded edges to make bag strap.

3. Insert one end of strap through brad ring and fold back 1" to underside of strap. Sew through all layers to secure strap (**Diagram 6**). Repeat with remaining strap end and brad ring.

add magnetic closure

Turn under edge of green print 2"-diameter circle; baste. Blanket-stitch fabric circle to center top of light green print lining, ¼" from edge, leaving a 1" opening at top.

Insert one half of magnetic snap closure into fabric circle pocket; blanket-stitch circle closed (see photo, *opposite right*). Repeat with remaining green print circle and other half of closure on opposite side of lining.

assemble removable bag liner

1. Sew together long edges of clear vinyl 10×16" rectangles to make a liner rectangle.

2. Fold liner rectangle in half on seam line; sew together side edges.

3. Repeat Assemble Bag, Step 4, on *page 18* to shape bottom corners of bag liner. Do not turn bag liner right side out.

4. Referring to **Diagram 7**, trim top edges of bag liner in a slight V-shape. Insert liner into bag.

COLOR OPTION

see clearly
The removable clear vinyl liner makes swapping bags a cinch. Make several bags in your favorite fabrics, plus one liner, then you'll easily be able to transfer all your essentials from bag to bag.

Make a sparkling tote that goes everywhere and holds everything.

daisydazzler

DESIGNER **M'LISS RAE HAWLEY**
PHOTOGRAPHER **CAMERON SADEGHPOUR**

materials

- ¼ yard bright pink print (bag center)
- 6×11" rectangle pink-and-orange dot (bag center)
- ⅜ yard pink-and-orange floral (bag center)
- ⅓ yard orange print (bag sides)
- ⅞ yard pink floral (bag lining, pockets, straps)
- ¼ yard pink print (bag lining)
- ⅛ yard batting (bag straps)
- 2⅝ yards lightweight fusible interfacing (such as Shape Flex)
- ¼ yard stiff interfacing (such as Timtex or Peltex)
- Magnetic snap closure
- Sequins and seed beads: assorted clear, pink, orange (optional)
- Long beading needle
- Beading thread

Finished bag: 13×12×10" (without straps)

Quantities are for 44/45"-wide, 100% cotton fabrics.
Measurements include ¼" seam allowances. Sew with right sides together unless otherwise stated.

cut fabrics

Cut pieces in the following order. Corner Cutting Pattern is on *page 25*.

From bright pink print, cut:
- 2—5¾×7½" A rectangles

From pink-and-orange dot, cut:
- 2—5¾×5½" B rectangles

From pink-and-orange floral, cut:
- 2—12½" C squares

From orange print, cut:
- 2—10½×13¾" D rectangles

From pink floral, cut:
- 2—2½×24" strips
- 2—15¾×22½" F rectangles
- 2—9×13" pocket rectangles
- 4—½×1" rectangles

From pink print, cut:
- 2—2¼×22½" E rectangles

From batting, cut:
- 2—1×24" strips

From lightweight fusible interfacing, cut:
- 2—2½×24" strips
- 2—15¾×22½" F rectangles
- 2—2¼×22½" E rectangles
- 2—12½" C squares
- 2—10½×13¾" D rectangles
- 2—6½×9" rectangles
- 2—5¾×7½" A rectangles
- 2—5¾×5½" B rectangles

From stiff interfacing, cut:
- 1—8½×11½" rectangle

editor's tip

Match thread and fabric colors when you want the topstitching to blend in with the fabric. When you want to accentuate the topstitching, choose a thread color that contrasts with the fabric color.

assemble bag center

1. Following manufacturer's instructions, fuse an A interfacing rectangle to wrong side of each bright pink print A rectangle. Then fuse an interfacing B rectangle to wrong side of each pink-and-orange dot B rectangle, and an interfacing C square to wrong side of each pink-and-orange floral C square.

2. Referring to **Diagram 1**, sew together a fused bright pink print A rectangle and a fused pink-and-orange dot B rectangle to make a bag unit; press seam toward bright pink print rectangle. Topstitch ⅛" from seam line.

3. Sew bag unit to a fused pink-and-orange floral C square; press seam toward large square. Topstitch ⅛" from seam line to make bag front (**Diagram 2**).

4. Repeat steps 2 and 3 to make a matching bag back.

5. Layer bag front and back with right sides together. Sew together along short bottom edges to make bag center. Using tip of iron, carefully press seam open (**Diagram 3**).

6. Sew a pink floral ½×1" rectangle ½" from short edge at one corner of stiff interfacing 8½×11½" rectangle to make a joining tab (**Diagram 4**). Repeat with remaining ½×1" rectangles to add tabs at all corners. (Tabs hold interfacing in place minimizing bulk in seams.) Center and baste interfacing rectangle over opened seam with tabs extending to long edges of bag center (**Diagram 5**). Working from right side of bag center, topstitch interfacing ⅛" from seam (**Diagram 6**).

7. If desired, hand-stitch assorted seed beads and sequins to printed fabrics on bag front and back using a long beading needle and two strands of matching beading thread.

add bag sides

1. Fuse an interfacing D rectangle to wrong side of each orange print D rectangle to make side panel pieces.

2. Using Corner Cutting Pattern, mark curved cutting line on each side panel piece to round off bottom corners. Trim along line (**Diagram 7**).

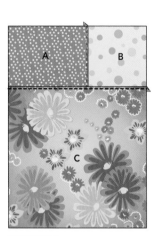

DIAGRAM 1

DIAGRAM 2

DIAGRAM 3

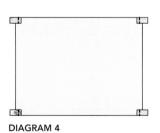

DIAGRAM 4

DIAGRAM 5

3. Referring to **Diagram 7**, fold a side panel in half lengthwise and pin-mark lower center. Matching bag center bottom seam and side panel lower center, join pieces, easing bag center around rounded corners of side panel and securing tabs on interfacing in seam (**Diagram 8**). Repeat with remaining bag center and side panel to make bag body.

4. Turn and press top edge of bag body ½" to wrong side. Turn bag body right side out.

assemble straps

1. Center a 2½×24" interfacing strip on wrong side of a pink floral 2½×24" strip; fuse.

2. Fold and press fused pink floral strip in half lengthwise with wrong side inside.

DIAGRAM 6

DIAGRAM 7

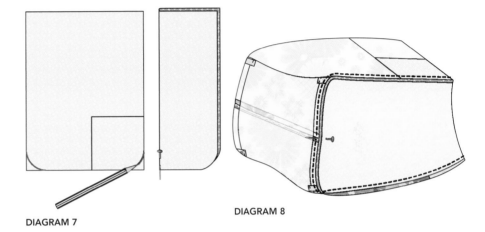

DIAGRAM 8

styled to suit

Sew with your favorite fabrics to make a Daisy Dazzler bag that's totally you. Paisleys and prints were used to stitch up a stylish patchwork option (*right*). Eye-catching bold prints in greens and browns were used for a more contemporary look (*below*).

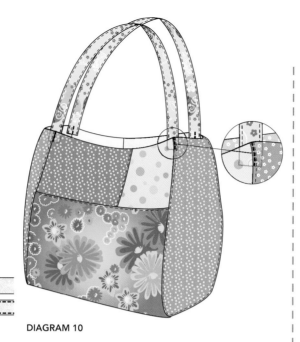

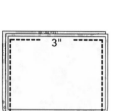

DIAGRAM 9

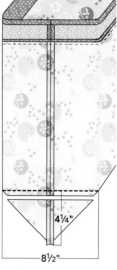

DIAGRAM 10

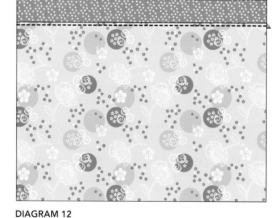

DIAGRAM 11

DIAGRAM 12

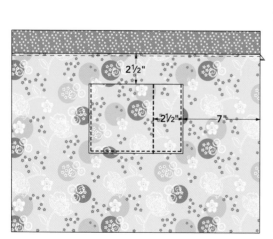

2½"

2½" ◄──── 7" ────►

DIAGRAM 13

4¼"

8½"

DIAGRAM 14

3. Open and press long edges ¼" to wrong side. Refold in half and press. Insert a 1×24" batting strip into fold. Topstitch ⅛" from outer edges to make a strap (**Diagram 9**).

4. Repeat steps 1–3 to make a second strap.

5. Referring to **Diagram 10**, center and pin one end of a strap under bag side seam. Stitch in the ditch to secure strap to bag. Repeat with opposite end of strap at remaining seam of same side of bag. Repeat with second strap on remaining side of bag.

assemble pockets and lining

1. Fold a pink floral 9×13" rectangle in half with right side inside to form a 6½×9" rectangle. Fuse a 6½×9" interfacing rectangle to wrong side of folded rectangle.

2. Sew folded rectangle along three open edges, leaving a 3" opening in long edge (**Diagram 11**). Turn right side out through opening and press flat to make a pocket piece. Turn under raw edges at opening; hand-stitch opening closed.

3. Repeat steps 1 and 2 to make a second pocket piece.

4. Fuse an interfacing E rectangle to wrong side of each pink print E rectangle and an interfacing F rectangle to wrong side of each pink floral F rectangle.

5. Referring to **Diagram 12**, sew together a fused pink print E rectangle and a fused pink floral F rectangle along long edges; press seam toward pink floral rectangle. Topstitch ⅛" from seam line to make a lining unit. Repeat to make a second lining unit.

6. Referring to **Diagram 13**, position a pocket piece on right side of a lining unit; pin in place. Edgestitch pocket piece to lining unit along pocket's side and bottom edges; leave top edge open. Stitch pocket divider (**Diagram 13**).

7. Join lining units along side and bottom edges to make lining body.

8. To shape flat bottom for lining, at one corner match bottom seam line to side seam line, creating a flattened triangle (**Diagram 14**). Measuring 4¼" from point of triangle, draw an 8½" line across triangle. Sew on drawn line. Trim excess fabric. Repeat with remaining bottom corner to make bag lining.

9. Turn and press top edge of bag lining ½" to wrong side. Do not turn right side out.

10. Referring to manufacturer's instructions, center and attach magnetic snap closure to right side of bag lining 1" from folded edge.

finish bag

1. Mark top center of bag side edge. Fold over 1" on both sides of center mark to make two pleats (**Diagram 15**). Baste in place. Repeat to make pleats at opposite bag side.

2. Mark lining top 2¼" from seam in both directions. Fold under lining 1" at each mark to make two pleats (**Diagram 16**). Baste in place. Repeat to make two pleats at opposite side of lining.

3. Insert lining into bag body with wrong sides together, aligning folded top edges.

4. Topstitch bag body and lining together ⅛" and ¼" from top edge to complete bag.

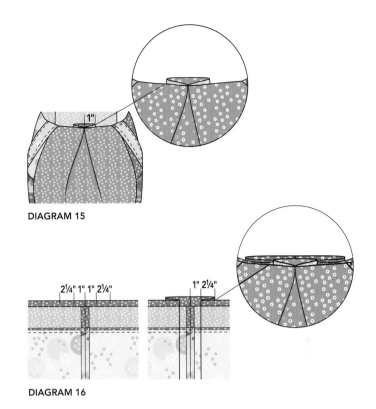

DIAGRAM 15

DIAGRAM 16

Daisy Dazzler
Corner Cutting Pattern

favorite CLUTCH

Make a statement with this curvy purse made in your favorite floral fabric.

DESIGNER **AMY BUTLER**
PHOTOGRAPHER **GREG SCHEIDEMANN**

materials

- ½ yard green floral (body, tab)
- ½ yard coordinating print (lining)
- ½ yard canvas (interlining)
- ½ yard of 13"-wide ultraheavyweight interfacing
- 1¼" of ¾"-wide sew-on hook-and-loop tape
- Fabric marker
- Pressing ham (optional; available at fabric or sewing stores)
- Vintage pin

Finished clutch: 11¾×7½"

Quantities are for 44/45"-wide, 100% cotton fabrics.
Measurements include ½" seam allowances. Sew with right sides together unless otherwise stated.

A sparkly antique pin at the tab closure accentuates the feminine shape of this sophisticated handheld purse.

cut fabrics

Cut pieces in the following order. Patterns are on *Pattern Sheet 1.* To make templates of the patterns, see Make and Use Templates, *page 158.*

Note: When cutting the clutch body and tab pieces (A, B, and D), you may wish to align patterns carefully to match fabric motifs.

From green floral, cut:
- 1 *each* of patterns A, B, and D

From coordinating print, cut:
- 1 *each* of patterns A, B, and D

From canvas, cut:
- 1 *each* of patterns A, B, and D

From ultraheavyweight interfacing, cut:
- 2 of Pattern C

editor's tip

Make the inside of your purse as beautiful as the exterior by constructing the lining from a small floral print. Picking fabrics from the same fabric collection ensures the fabrics will go together beautifully.

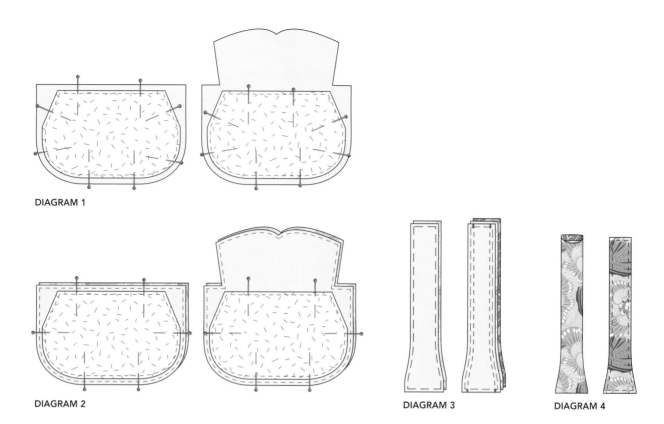

DIAGRAM 1

DIAGRAM 2

DIAGRAM 3

DIAGRAM 4

assemble clutch body

1. Referring to **Diagram 1**, center an interfacing C piece atop wrong side of canvas A piece, leaving ½" of canvas exposed around outer edges; pin. *Note: Interfacing pieces are cut smaller than canvas pieces to reduce bulk in seam allowances and to make it easier to shape sides of clutch.*

2. Sew ¼" inside edges of interfacing to make a front interfacing unit.

3. Repeat steps 1 and 2 to sew remaining interfacing C piece atop wrong side of canvas B piece to make a back interfacing unit.

4. Referring to **Diagram 2**, align front interfacing unit, canvas side down, atop wrong side of green floral A piece; pin. Machine-baste ¼" from outer edges to make clutch front.

5. Repeat Step 4 to sew back interfacing unit atop wrong side of green floral B piece to make clutch back.

assemble and add tab

The tab on this clutch serves as both a handle on clutch back side (see photo, *opposite, left*) and as a closure.

1. Layer canvas D piece on wrong side of green floral D piece; baste ¼" from outer edge (**Diagram 3**).

2. With right sides together, layer Step 1 unit and coordinating print (lining) D piece. Backstitching at the beginning and end, sew together long edges, using a ½" seam to make tab; leave short edges open for turning (**Diagram 3**).

3. Trim seam allowances to ⅛". Turn tab right side out by pulling narrow end through wide end; press.

4. Tuck ½" of wide end inside tab; press. Tuck ⅜" of narrow end inside (**Diagram 4**); press. Topstitch around tab, ¼" from outer edge.

5. Referring to **Diagram 5**, center and sew hook portion of hook-and-loop tape to tab lining side, ¼" from wide end.

6. Fold clutch back in half lengthwise and finger-press a crease for a placement line. Unfold clutch back.

7. Referring to **Diagram 6**, mark a placement line 3½" above lower edge of clutch back on right side. With right sides together, center narrow end of tab over center crease along marked placement line. Backstitching at the beginning and end, edgestitch across narrow end, then again ½" from edgestitching.

8. Referring to **Diagram 7**, fold tab over clutch back. With 1" of tab extending toward bottom of bag, fold tab back on itself and up, centering it over center crease. Press and pin. The wide edge of the tab will extend past upper edge. Mark and sew across tab 5½" above bottom folded edge, backstitching at each edge to make a handle on clutch back; press.

DIAGRAM 5

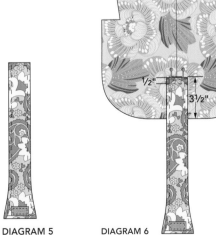

½"

3½"

DIAGRAM 6

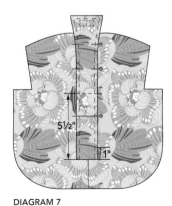

5½"

1"

DIAGRAM 7

editor's tip

If you can't find a vintage pin that suits your style, consider gluing a pin back to a retro earring or substituting a hand-cast clay or metal one-of-a-kind button.

assemble clutch

1. Fold clutch front in half widthwise and finger-press a crease for a placement line. Unfold clutch front.

2. Mark a placement line on clutch front 5" below upper edge at center fold (**Diagram 8**). Center and edgestitch loop portion of hook-and-loop tape to clutch front right side, just below marked line.

3. With right sides together, align side and lower edges of clutch front and clutch back; pin. Using a ½" seam allowance, sew together along side and lower edges (**Diagram 9**).

4. Trim seam allowance around bottom curves to ¼". Press seam open using a pressing ham, if desired. Turn right side out; press. *Note: Pressing seam open creates a crisp, finished look around curves at clutch bottom.*

5. Repeat steps 3 and 4 with coordinating print (lining) A and B pieces to make clutch lining.

6. With right side of clutch body facing in and wrong side of clutch lining facing out, place clutch body inside clutch lining, aligning side seams (**Diagram 10**). Pin together raw edges, making sure tab is tucked in between clutch body and lining, out of the way. Using a ½" seam allowance, sew together raw

DIAGRAM 8

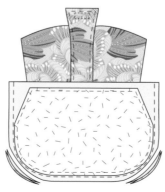

DIAGRAM 9

DIAGRAM 10

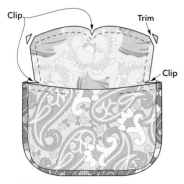

DIAGRAM 11

DIAGRAM 12

DIAGRAM 13

DIAGRAM 14

edges, leaving a 5" opening for turning in center front.

7. Trim seam allowance across points of clutch back, making sure not to clip into stitching. Referring to **Diagram 11**, clip into seam allowance just to stitching line at corners where bag flap extends from clutch back. Clip into seam allowance at center top of clutch back.

8. Turn clutch right side out through 5" opening. Push lining down inside clutch, aligning side seams; press upper edges. To close opening, topstitch ⅛" from open edges of clutch (**Diagram 12**).

finish clutch

1. On one side, match side seams on clutch body with lining; pin.

With clutch body facing up, start at top finished edge on side seam and stitch in the ditch 3½" down (**Diagram 13**). Repeat on other side of clutch body.

2. To give the clutch shape, fold a 1¼" angled pleat into one side seam, beginning at the top and tapering pleat to end 3½" down (**Diagram 14**). Press folds in place. Repeat on remaining side seam. *Note:* The absence of ultraheavyweight interfacing in the area you're pleating should enable you to make crisp folds.

3. Attach a vintage pin onto right side of tab's wide end, covering stitching where hook-and-loop tape was sewn.

4. Fold clutch back over clutch front, aligning hook-and-loop closures, to complete clutch.

This personalized fabric portfolio sports a front pocket and zippered pouch large enough for valuable papers and files.

style file

DESIGNER **KAREN MONTGOMERY**
PHOTOGRAPHERS **GREG SCHEIDEMANN**
AND JASON DONNELLY

materials

- ⅓ yard total assorted batik scraps (pocket)

- ½ yard orange batik (portfolio back, lining, pocket lining)

- ½ yard mottled deep rose (portfolio front)

- ½ yard cotton flannel (interlining)

- 20"-long zipper

- Zipper pull

Finished portfolio: 11×14"

Quantities are for 44/45"-wide fabrics.
Measurements include ½" seam allowances. Sew with right sides together unless otherwise stated.

An eye-catching portfolio with panache comes in handy for toting and storing papers and notes.

cut fabrics

Cut pieces in the following order.

From assorted batik scraps, cut:
- 7—3×17" strips

From orange batik, cut:
- 1—15×26" rectangle
- 1—9½×15" rectangle

From mottled deep rose, cut:
- 1—15×21" rectangle

From flannel, cut:
- 1—13×15" rectangle
- 1—11×15" rectangle
- 1—9×15" rectangle

assemble strip-pieced pocket

1. Cut assorted batik 3×17" strips into uneven strips. Our strips measure 1⅞" wide at one end, 2½" to 3" wide at opposite end.

2. Sew strips together into a pieced rectangle (**Diagram 1**). Trim pieced rectangle to 9½×15" including seam allowances.

3. Join pieced rectangle and orange batik 9½×15" rectangle along one long edge. Turn to right side. Press. Insert flannel 9×15" rectangle between folded fabric layers. Topstitch ¼" from folded edge to secure flannel. Topstitch pieced strips. Trim flannel even with fabric edges to make pocket.

editor's tip

Use wash-away basting tape or a water-soluble glue stick to hold zipper in place before securing it with machine stitching.

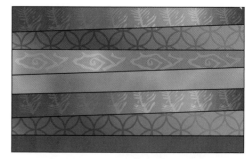

DIAGRAM 1

editor's tip

Got a favorite fabric you just can't bear to cut up?
Use a 9½×15" rectangle from one print, instead of
a pieced rectangle, for the pocket.

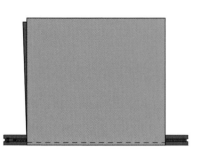

DIAGRAM 2   **DIAGRAM 3**   **DIAGRAM 4**

---

assemble portfolio

1. Fold and press mottled deep
   rose 15×21" rectangle in half,
   making a 15×10½" rectangle.
   Place closed zipper inside folded
   mottled deep rose rectangle,
   allowing ends of zipper to extend
   beyond fabric (**Diagram 2**).
   Pin zipper in place,
   aligning one edge
   of zipper tape
   along fold.

2. Sew ¼" to ⅜" from fold to secure
   zipper. *Note:* The closer you sew
   to the zipper, the less of it will
   show on the finished project. Be
   careful not to sew too close to
   zipper teeth so the fabric won't
   catch in the zipper.

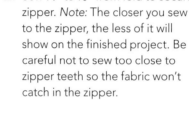

3. Open folded rectangle and fold
   wrong sides together to expose
   zipper as shown in **Diagram 3**.

4. Fold and press orange batik
   15×26" rectangle in half to make
   a 15×13" rectangle. Place zipper
   unit inside orange batik rectangle,
   aligning remaining zipper tape
   edge along fold (**Diagram 4**). Pin
   in place and sew along fold as
   previously done. Open folded
   rectangle and fold it, wrong sides
   together, to expose zipper.

5. Insert flannel 13×15" rectangle
   between orange batik layers.
   Topstitch ¼" from folded edge
   to hold flannel in place. Insert
   flannel 11×15" rectangle between
   mottled deep rose layers.
   Topstitch to make zippered unit
   (**Diagram 5**).

6. Quilt as desired. Trim flannel
   even with fabric edges.

7. Place pocket on mottled deep
   rose section of zippered unit,
   aligning bottom edges
   (**Diagram 6**). Baste in place
   by hand or machine.

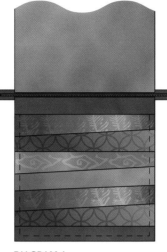

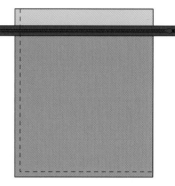

DIAGRAM 5

DIAGRAM 6

DIAGRAM 7

8. Fold zippered unit in half, matching raw edges; pin in place. Sew together side edge with zipper tail and across bottom of unit (**Diagram 7**). Do NOT sew side with zipper tab. (If you have a serger you can serge the side and bottom seam and trim the zipper—all in one step.)

9. Open zipper, moving tab to tail end inside Step 8 unit. Sew or serge remaining side edge (**Diagram 8**). Trim seams, including excess zipper tape, with pinking shears, or zigzag-stitch edges to prevent fabric fraying. Turn portfolio right side out and press. Attach zipper pull.

DIAGRAM 8

COLOR OPTION

tennis anyone?

You can create dramatically different versions of "Style File" by varying the fabric selections. In this version, a tennis-theme print is teamed up with a bold gold print and solid black. A row of machine-quilted featherstitches embellishes the edge of the second pocket piece.

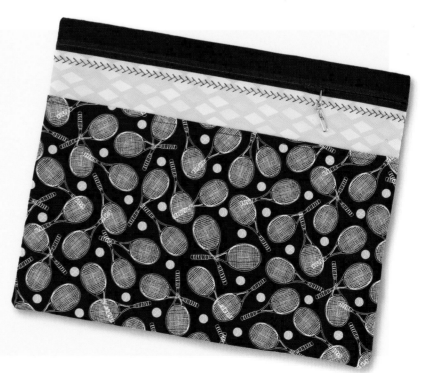

This easy-to-sew tote makes shopping even more fun. Change fabrics for a seasonal look, or choose prints in colors to showcase team spirit.

market bag

DESIGNER **JOANNA FIGUEROA OF FIG TREE & CO.**
PHOTOGRAPHERS **GREG SCHEIDEMANN AND MARTY BALDWIN**

materials

- 24—5" squares assorted purple, pink, and gold prints (front and back)
- ¼ yard gold print (sides and bottom)
- ¼ yard brown print (handles)
- ⅔ yard beige print (lining)
- ⅔ yard muslin
- ¾ yard batting

Finished bag: 17½×13½×4" (without handle)

Quantities are for 44/45"-wide, 100% cotton fabrics.
Measurements include ¼" seam allowances. Sew with right sides together unless otherwise stated.

Mix and match your favorite fabrics to make this roomy tote with patchwork sides.

cut fabrics

Cut pieces in the following order. Corner Cutting Pattern is on *page 39*. To make a template of the pattern, see Make and Use Templates, *page 158*.

From gold print, cut:
- 1—4½×42" strip
From brown print, cut:
- 2—4¾×19½" strips
From beige print, cut:
- 2—16×22½" rectangles
From muslin, cut:
- 1—4½×42" strip
- 2—14×18½" rectangles
From batting, cut:
- 1—4½×42" strip
- 2—2×19½" strips
- 2—14×18½" rectangles

assemble and quilt bag body

1. Referring to photo, *opposite*, lay out twelve 5" squares in three rows. Sew together squares in each row. Press seams in one direction, alternating direction with each row. Join rows to make bag front. Press seams in one direction. Bag front should be 18½×14" including seam allowances.

2. Layer bag front with batting and muslin 18½×14" rectangles. (For details, see Complete the Quilt, *page 160*.) Baste layers a scant ¼" from all edges. Quilt as desired.

3. Repeat steps 1 and 2 using remaining 5" squares to make bag back.

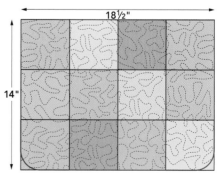

DIAGRAM 1

4. Using Corner Cutting Pattern, mark cutting line on bag front and back pieces for rounding bottom corners (**Diagram 1**, *page 36*). Machine-baste a scant ¼" inside line. Trim along line.

5. Mark center of bag front along top edge. Fold over ¾" on both sides of center mark to make two pleats (**Diagram 2**). Baste in place. Repeat to make pleats in bag back.

6. Layer gold print 4½×42" strip with batting and muslin 4½×42" strips; baste. Quilt as desired to make bag side/bottom strip.

7. With right sides together and aligning raw edges, sew together bag front and bag side/bottom strip. Press seam open. Join bag back to remaining raw edge of side/bottom strip to make bag body.

assemble and quilt handles

1. Fold under ½" along one long edge of a brown print 4¾×19½" (**Diagram 3**); press.

2. Fold the same edge under 1" (**Diagram 4**); press. Open up the last fold and align a 2×19½" batting strip with the fold line (**Diagram 5**).

3. Fold long raw edge of brown print strip over batting. Then refold other long edge on fold line; pin in place.

4. Referring to **Diagram 6**, stitch down center to secure folded edge. Stitch on both sides of centerline, ¼" to ⅜" apart.

5. Fold handle in half crosswise to find center; mark with a pin.

Fold handle in half lengthwise and pin 2½" on both sides of center (**Diagram 7**). Stitch folded edges together for 5" to make a narrower portion of the handle, which is more comfortable to carry.

6. Repeat steps 1–5 to make a second handle.

assemble bag lining

1. Repeat Assemble and Quilt Outer Bag, Step 5, using beige print 16×22½" rectangles to make pleats in lining rectangles.

2. Layer lining rectangles right sides together. Sew together side and bottom edges, leaving a 5" opening on one side for turning bag right side out. Press seams open.

3. To shape a flat bottom for lining, at one corner, match bottom seam line to side seam line, creating a flattened triangle (**Diagram 8**). Measure and mark on seam allowance 2½" from point of triangle. Draw a 4"-long line across triangle and sew on drawn line. Trim excess fabric. Repeat at remaining bottom corner to make bag lining. Leave lining wrong side out.

finish bag

1. Referring to **Diagram 9**, pin handle ends to bag front and back 1¼" in from side edges. Attach handles, stitching through all layers a scant ¼" from edges.

2. With right sides together, insert bag body inside bag lining; the handles should be between the bag and lining. Align raw edges and pleats. Stitch together top

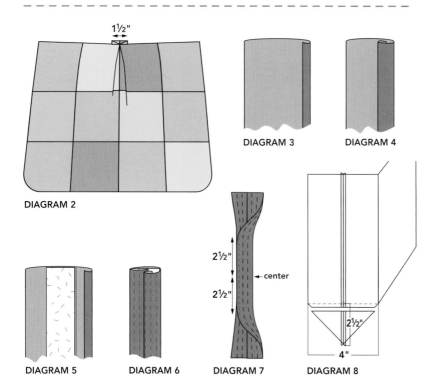

DIAGRAM 2

DIAGRAM 3

DIAGRAM 4

DIAGRAM 5

DIAGRAM 6

DIAGRAM 7

DIAGRAM 8

spring tote

Sweet pink and cream mini florals and prints welcome spring in this version of the Market Bag. A great overnight tote or on-the-go bag for kids' games, toys, and blankets, this easy-to-sew project is roomy. Add a fabric loop and button to secure the top, or check out other unique fasteners available at crafts and sewing stores.

edges of bag body and lining, backstitching over each handle for reinforcement.

3. Turn bag and lining right side out through opening in lining; then pull the lining out of the bag. Machine-stitch opening in lining closed.

4. Insert lining back into bag and press top edge. Topstitch ¼" from top edge to complete bag.

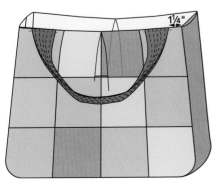

DIAGRAM 9

Market Bag
Corner Cutting Pattern

Grab it and go! A petite and stylish shoulder bag, with divided pockets inside, organizes all the essentials you need for a day full of shopping fun.

shop hopper's BAG

DESIGNER **SHERRI K. FALLS**
PHOTOGRAPHERS **CAMERON SADEGHPOUR AND MARTY BALDWIN**

materials

- 18×22" piece (fat quarter) green batik (lining)
- 18×22" piece (fat quarter) dark purple batik (bag body)
- ⅓ yard light purple batik (pockets, handle)
- 18×22" piece (fat quarter) blue batik (binding, covered button)
- 8½×15½" batting
- 1×37" cotton webbing (handle)
- 1"-diameter button to cover
- ⅝×1" piece hook-and-loop tape

Finished bag: 6×8" (without handle)

Quantities are for 44/45"-wide, 100% cotton fabrics.
Measurements include ¼" seam allowances. Sew with right sides together unless otherwise stated.

cut fabrics

Cut pieces in the following order. Corner Cutting Pattern is on *Pattern Sheet 1.* To make template of pattern, see Make and Use Templates, *page 158.*

From *each* green and dark purple batik, cut:
- 1—8½×15½" rectangle

From light purple batik, cut:
- 1—4×38" strip
- 2—4½×8" strips

From blue batik, cut:
- Enough 2½"-wide bias strips to total 55" for binding (For details, see Cutting Bias Strips, *page 159.*)
- 1—2" square

quilt bag body

1. Lay green batik 8½×15½" lining rectangle right side down on a flat surface. Aligning edges, place 8½×15½" batting rectangle on top. Place dark purple batik 8½×15½" rectangle right side up on top of batting. Baste. (For details, see Complete the Quilt, *page 160.*)

2. Quilt as desired, then trim quilted rectangle to 8×15". The rectangle shown (**Diagram 1**) was machine-quilted with parallel lines about 1" apart.

3. Using Corner Cutting Pattern, mark cutting line on top corners of quilted rectangle for rounding flap corners (**Diagram 1**).

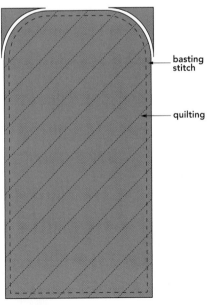

basting stitch

quilting

DIAGRAM 1

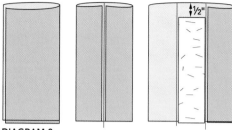

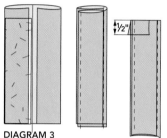

DIAGRAM 2

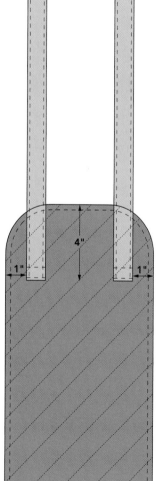

DIAGRAM 3

Machine-baste a scant ⅛" inside line and all edges. Trim along cutting line to make bag body.

assemble and attach handle

1. Fold light purple batik 4×38" strip in half, wrong side inside. Press, then unfold. Fold long edges to meet in center; press again (**Diagram 2**).

2. Open one long edge and place 1×37" cotton webbing strip inside along fold line (**Diagram 2**). *Note:* Webbing will be ½" shorter than fabric on each end.

3. Refold long edge toward center of strip. Referring to **Diagram 3**, fold in half lengthwise, matching folded edges, and press. Topstitch along both long edges. Fold ends in about ½" and press to make handle.

4. Referring to **Diagram 4**, pin handle ends to outside of bag body 4" down from top edge and 1" in from both side edges. *Note:* Raw, turned-under ends of handle should face bag body.

5. Machine-stitch each handle end in a rectangle to secure handle to bag.

add pockets

1. With right side inside, fold light purple batik 4½×8" strip in half lengthwise. Press. Strip now should be 2¼×8". Machine-stitch long edges (**Diagram 5**). Turn right side out and press to make a pocket rectangle. Repeat to make a second pocket rectangle.

2. Pin one pocket rectangle 3½" down from bag top on lining side (**Diagram 6**). Stitch along bottom edge through all layers.

3. Pin remaining pocket rectangle 4" down from bag top (**Diagram 7**). Stitch as before.

DIAGRAM 5

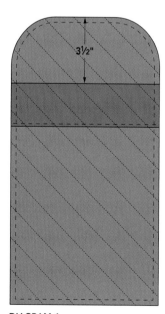

DIAGRAM 4

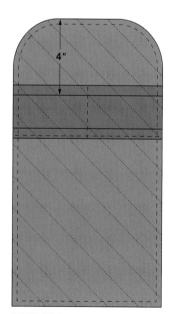

DIAGRAM 6

DIAGRAM 7

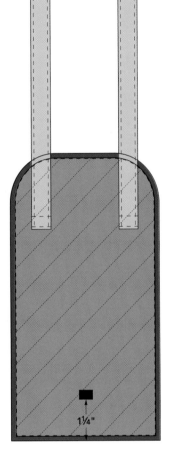

DIAGRAM 8

DIAGRAM 9

4. Stitch vertically through center of pocket rectangles to create four small pockets. *Note:* Side edges will be stitched later.

finish bag

1. Bind bag body with blue batik bias binding strips. (For details, see Better Binding, *page 160*.)

2. Referring to **Diagram 8,** center and stitch one part of hook-and-loop tape to inside of flap ¾" from edge. Center and stitch remaining part of hook-and-loop tape to outside of bag 1¼" from opposite edge.

3. Fold bottom edge of bag up 6" with pockets inside (**Diagram 9**). Stitch bag sides in the ditch along binding.

4. Following manufacturer's directions, cover button using blue batik 2" square.

5. Center button on outside of flap about ¾" from edge; hand-stitch button in place (covering stitches that secure hook-and-loop tape) to complete bag.

on the GO

DESIGNER **CINDY TAYLOR OATES**
PHOTOGRAPHER **ADAM ALBRIGHT**

Sew this attractive laptop bag for a friend, then reward yourself by making one to keep.

materials

- ½ yard green large print (bag)
- ¾ yard green small print (flap, lining)
- ½ yard blue print (piping)
- ¾ yard muslin (backing)
- 2—17×13" rectangles batting
- 17×9" rectangle batting
- 1 yard ³⁄₁₆"-diameter cording
- 1¼"-diameter button
- Basting spray (optional)

Finished bag: 12×16"

Quantities are for 44/45"-wide, 100% cotton fabrics.
Measurements include ¼" seam allowances. Sew with right sides together unless otherwise stated.

Colorful piping edges the flap of this portable computer bag. If making or adding piping is new to you, this is a great starter project. Neither is difficult—you make the piping from bias fabric strips and purchased cording, and then stitch it with a zipper foot onto the curved edge of the flap before assembling the bag.

cut fabrics

Cut pieces in the following order. Flap Pattern is on *Pattern Sheet 1.*

From green large print, cut:
- 2—17×13" rectangles

From green small print, cut:
- 2—16½×12½" rectangles
- 1—17×9" rectangle
- 1 of Flap Pattern for lining

From blue print, cut:
- 1—1½×29" bias strip for piping (For details, see Cutting Bias Strips, *page 159.*)
- 1—1×3" bias strip for button loop

From muslin, cut:
- 2—17×13" rectangles
- 1—17×9" rectangle

quilt bag body pieces

1. Layer a green large print 17×13" rectangle, 17×13" batting rectangle, and 17×13" muslin rectangle. Spray-baste or pin to hold layers in place. Using matching thread, machine-quilt as desired. (Ours features a meandering pattern machine-quilted across the rectangle.) Trim quilted rectangle to 16½×12½" to make a bag body piece. Repeat to make a second bag body piece.

2. Layer green small print 17×9" rectangle, 17×9" batting rectangle, and 17×9" muslin rectangle. Spray-baste or pin; machine-quilt as before to make quilted rectangle. Using Flap Pattern, cut flap from quilted rectangle.

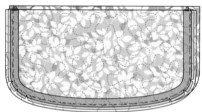

DIAGRAM 1

DIAGRAM 2

DIAGRAM 3

DIAGRAM 4

make piping

Fold blue print 1½×29" bias strip in half lengthwise, wrong side inside; press. Insert ³⁄₁₆"-wide cording in fold. Using a long basting stitch and machine-cording foot or zipper foot, sew as close to cording as possible to make piping. Trim seam allowance to ¼".

assemble flap

1. Aligning raw edges and using a cording or zipper foot, stitch piping to right side of quilted flap's curved edge. Clip seam allowance of piping at curves (**Diagram 1**).

2. With wrong side inside, fold blue print 1×3" bias strip in half lengthwise; press. Open strip and press long edges to center. Refold in half and press. Topstitch along double-fold edge to make button loop.

3. Aligning raw edges, sew loop ends to flap center ¼" from edge; press (**Diagram 2**).

4. With right sides together and using the piping basting line as a guide, sew together quilted flap and green small print flap lining just inside basting (**Diagram 3**).

5. Clip curves. Turn flap right side out; press flat.

6. Topstitch ¼" from finished edge and a scant ⅛" from raw edge of flap (**Diagram 4**).

assemble outer bag

1. With right sides together, join bag body pieces along three edges (**Diagram 5**). Clip corners; turn right side out and press to make outer bag.

2. With right sides together, sew long edge of flap to one edge of outer bag ⅛" from raw edges (**Diagram 6**).

DIAGRAM 5

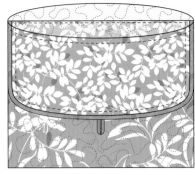

DIAGRAM 6

4"

DIAGRAM 7

editor's tip

Matching thread color to fabric or trim can give a more professional appearance; change thread color when you change fabric color.

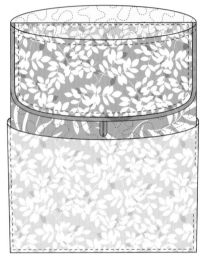

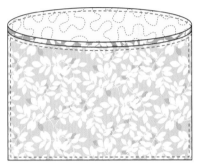

DIAGRAM 8

assemble lining and finish bag

1. With right sides together, join green small print 16½×12½" rectangles along bottom and side edges, leaving a 4" opening along one side for turning, to make bag lining (**Diagram 7**). Clip corners; press.

2. Insert outer bag into bag lining right sides together, matching seams; pin. Sew together outer bag and bag lining (**Diagram 8**).

3. Turn bag to right side through opening in lining. Slip-stitch opening closed. Insert lining into bag; press. Topstitch ¼" around upper edge of bag, keeping flap free (**Diagram 9**).

4. Center button 4¼" above lower edge of bag and sew in place through bag front to complete bag.

BAG BACK

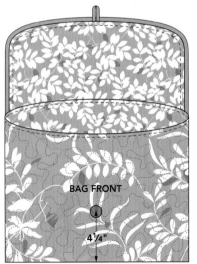

BAG FRONT

4¼"

DIAGRAM 9

DESIGNER **ANGELA PHILLIPS**
PHOTOGRAPHER **ANDY LYONS**

curve appeal

The secret to the structure of this shapely tote hides from view. It's fusible fleece.

materials

- 1 yard floral (bag body, pocket, straps)
- 1 yard multicolor stripe (bag body, bag base, bag lining, pocket trim, pockets)
- 1½ yards fusible fleece
- 6×14" ultrastiff plastic canvas

Finished bag: 12×14"

Quantities are for 44/45"-wide, 100% cotton fabrics.
Measurements include ¼" seam allowances. Sew with right sides together unless otherwise stated.

Choose a colorful floral and stripe to create this must-have carryall that includes pockets both outside and in for all your essential items.

cut fabrics

Cut pieces in the following order. Base Support Pattern is on *page 53*. Bag Body Cutting Pattern is on *Pattern Sheet 2*. To make templates of the patterns, see Make and Use Templates, *page 158*.

From brown floral, cut:
- 2—5×22½" strips
- 2—11½×18" rectangles
- 1—4½×5" rectangle

From multicolor stripe, cut:
- 2—15½×18" rectangles
- 2—4½×18" rectangles
- 2—7×16" rectangles
- 3—4½×7" rectangles
- 2—4½×5¾" rectangles

From fusible fleece, cut:
- 4—15½×18" rectangles
- 2—7×16" rectangles
- 2—5×22½" strips
- 1—4×6½" rectangle
- 1—4×5½" rectangle
- 1—4×5¼" rectangle

From plastic canvas, cut:
- 1 of Base Support Pattern

assemble and quilt

outer pocket

1. Join short edges of floral 4½×5" rectangle and a multicolor stripe 4½×7" rectangle to make pocket unit (**Diagram 1**). Press seam toward multicolor stripe.

2. Fold pocket unit in half, aligning short edges. Join side and lower edges, leaving a 3" opening for turning (**Diagram 2**).

DIAGRAM 1

DIAGRAM 2

Begin each project with a new sewing machine needle, or change it after every eight hours of sewing. A blunt needle can weaken seams or cause skipped stitches.

DIAGRAM 3

DIAGRAM 4

DIAGRAM 5

3. Trim across bottom corners of fleece 4×5½" rectangle to reduce bulk. Following manufacturer's instructions, fuse to wrong side of pocket unit (**Diagram 3**). Turn right side out through opening. Press and slip-stitch opening closed to make a pocket. Quilt as desired.

assemble and quilt bag body

1. Sew together a floral 11½×18" rectangle and a multicolor stripe 4½×18" rectangle to make pieced unit (**Diagram 4**). Press seam toward multicolor stripe.

2. Press fusible fleece 15½×18" rectangle to wrong side of pieced unit; let cool. Using Bag Body Cutting Pattern, cut out bag body piece. Quilt bag body piece as desired. Designer Angela Phillips used an allover stipple pattern to quilt the pieces for this bag.

3. Repeat steps 1 and 2 to make and quilt a second bag body piece.

4. Position pocket on one bag body piece (see Bag Body Cutting Pattern for placement). Topstitch side and bottom edges of pocket to bag body piece (**Diagram 5**).

5. Join side edges of bag body pieces. Press seams open. Align the side seams so they now meet at center of bag. Mark new side "seams" of bag body with pins (**Diagram 6**).

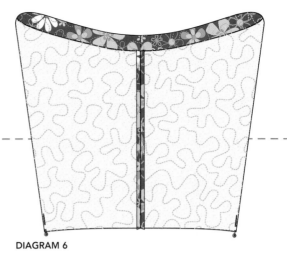

DIAGRAM 6

6. Press fusible fleece 7×16" rectangle to wrong side of each multicolor stripe 7×16" rectangle. Cut two of Bag Base Cutting Pattern from fused rectangles. Set one bag base aside for lining. Quilt one bag base as desired.

7. Fold bag base in fourths, and mark each fold with a pin. Matching quarter marks, sew together bag base and bag body to make outer bag (**Diagram 7**). Turn outer bag right side out.

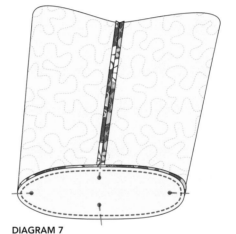

DIAGRAM 7

DIAGRAM 8

assemble straps

1. Press a fusible fleece 5×22½" strip to wrong side of a floral 5×22½" strip. With wrong side inside, fold fused strip in half. Press, then unfold. Fold long edges to meet in center; press again (**Diagram 8**).

2. Referring to **Diagram 8**, fold strip in half lengthwise, matching folded edges, and press. Topstitch along both edges and down the center to make a strap.

3. Repeat steps 1 and 2 to make a second strap.

4. Referring to **Diagram 9**, pin strap ends to outside of bag body, 2½" from seams. Align strap ends with upper curved edge; baste.

DIAGRAM 9

assemble lining

1. Join two multicolor stripe 4½×7" rectangles around all edges, leaving a 2½" opening along one edge, to make pocket unit.

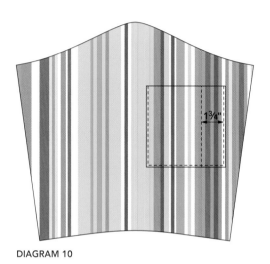

1¾"

DIAGRAM 10

2. Trim across corners of fleece 4×6½" rectangle and fuse to wrong side of pocket unit as previously done. Turn right side out through opening. Press and slip-stitch opening closed to make pocket.

3. Repeat steps 1 and 2 using multicolor stripe 4½×5¾" rectangles and fleece 4×5¼" rectangle to make a second pocket.

4. Press each remaining fusible fleece 15½×18" rectangle to wrong side of multicolor stripe 15½×18" rectangles. Using Bag Body Cutting Pattern, cut out two lining body pieces.

COLOR OPTION

color conscious

To make this version of Curve Appeal, project tester Judy Sams Sohn chose a blue-and-purple floral and a complementary stripe. The contrast between the two fabrics is subtle, but it makes a fashionable tote.

5. Position pockets on lining body pieces (see **Diagram 10** for placement). Topstitch pockets in place along side and lower edges. Stitch down large pocket 1¾" from edge to make a divided pocket (**Diagram 10**).

6. Sew together side edges of body lining pieces, leaving a 4" opening for turning.

7. Referring to Assemble and Quilt Bag Body, Step 7, mark and pin body lining pieces and remaining bag base. Sew together to make bag lining.

finish bag

1. Insert outer bag into bag lining with right sides together and seams matching. Stitch along top edges. Turn bag right side out through opening in lining. Smooth lining inside bag. Press bag's upper edge; topstitch ⅛" from edge.

2. Insert plastic canvas base support through the lining opening; fit in place at bottom of bag. Slip-stitch opening closed.

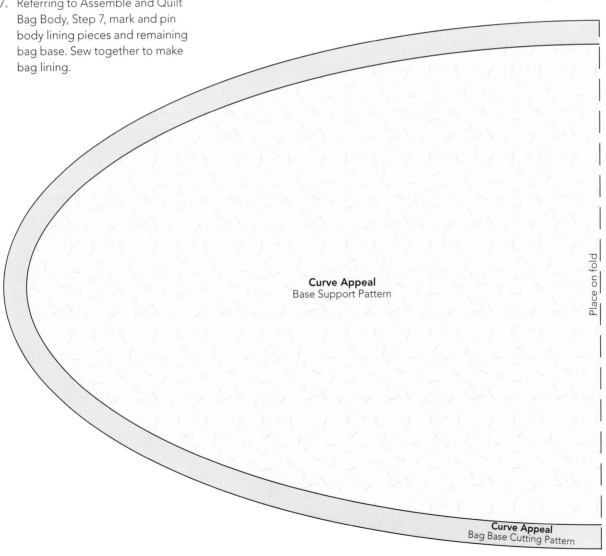

Curve Appeal
Base Support Pattern

Place on fold

Curve Appeal
Bag Base Cutting Pattern

Customize a spa bag by filling it with toiletries of your choosing to create a delightful token of affection.

OH SO *soothing*

DESIGNER **LESLIE GLADMAN**
PHOTOGRAPHERS **KRITSADA AND PERRY STRUSE**

materials

- ½ yard yellow paisley (bag)
- ⅜ yard blue print (lining)
- Scrap of batting
- 2⅓ yards narrow satin cording or ribbon
- 4—⅜"-diameter buttons
- 1 package 1"-wide single-fold bias tape

Finished bag: 12×9×8"

Quantities are for 44/45"-wide, 100% cotton fabrics.
Measurements include ¼" seam allowances. Sew with right sides together unless otherwise stated.

cut fabrics

Cut pieces in the following order. Patterns are on *pages 57–59.* To make templates of the patterns, see Make and Use Templates, *page 158.*

From yellow paisley, cut:
- 4 *each* of patterns A and B
- 1 of Pattern C

From blue print, cut:
- 4 of Pattern A
- 1 of Pattern C

From batting scrap, cut:
- 1 of Pattern C

From single-fold bias tape, cut:
- 4—5"-long pieces

assemble spa bag

1. With wrong side inside, fold each yellow paisley B piece in half; press. Referring to marked dots on full-size pattern piece for placement, make an inverted box pleat along bottom raw edges of each folded B piece; stitch in place to make four pocket units.

2. Place a pocket unit atop right side of a yellow paisley A piece. Machine-baste pocket unit raw edges to A piece to make a spa bag unit (**Diagram 1**). Repeat to make four spa bag units total.

3. Press under ½" at each end of 5"-long pieces of single-fold bias tape.

DIAGRAM 1

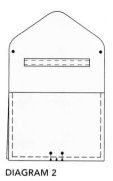

DIAGRAM 2

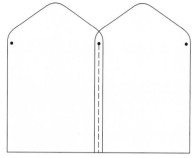

DIAGRAM 3

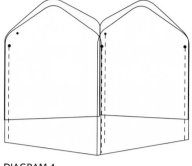

DIAGRAM 4

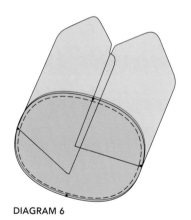

DIAGRAM 5

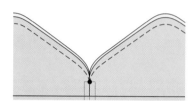

DIAGRAM 6

4. Referring to **Diagram 2**, place a pressed bias tape strip atop right side of each spa bag unit as marked on full-size pattern. Topstitch close to long edges of bias strips, leaving ends open.

5. Sew together spa bag units in pairs, starting at marked dots and finishing at bottom edges (**Diagram 3**). In the same manner, join the pairs to make a pocket tube (**Diagram 4**). Press open seam allowances. Turn right side out.

6. Sew together blue print A pieces in pairs, starting at marked dots and finishing at bottom edges. Press seams open. In the same manner, join pairs to make a lining tube. Press seams open.

7. Place pocket tube inside lining tube with right sides together. Join top edges, stitching carefully to marked dots (**Diagram 5**). Trim seam allowance to ⅛", clipping close to marked dots. Turn joined tubes right side out; press. Machine-baste around bottom raw edge of pocket/lining tube to secure layers together.

8. With wrong sides inside, layer batting C piece between yellow paisley C piece and blue print C piece; machine-baste to make bottom unit.

9. Matching arrows and seams of yellow paisley pieces, align pocket tube with bottom unit; sew together to make spa bag (**Diagram 6**). Turn bag right side out.

10. Stitch a button to each pocket intersection.

11. Cut cording in half and thread half through bias strips around bag. Knot ends together. Thread other cord half around bag in opposite direction and knot ends to complete spa bag.

12. Pull to draw up cords.

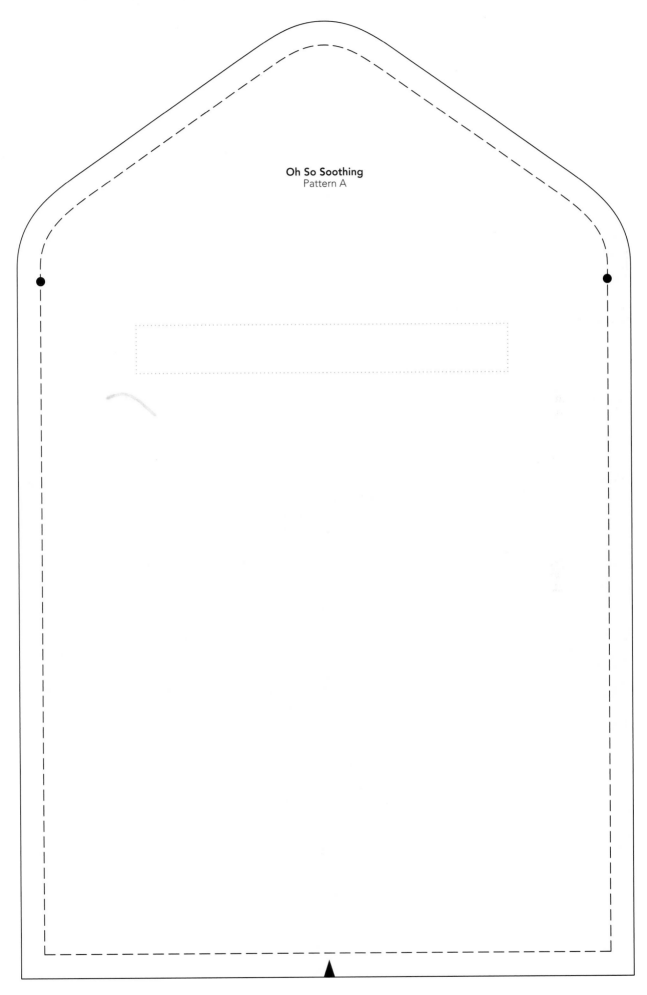

Oh So Soothing
Pattern A

Oh So Soothing
Pattern B

Fold

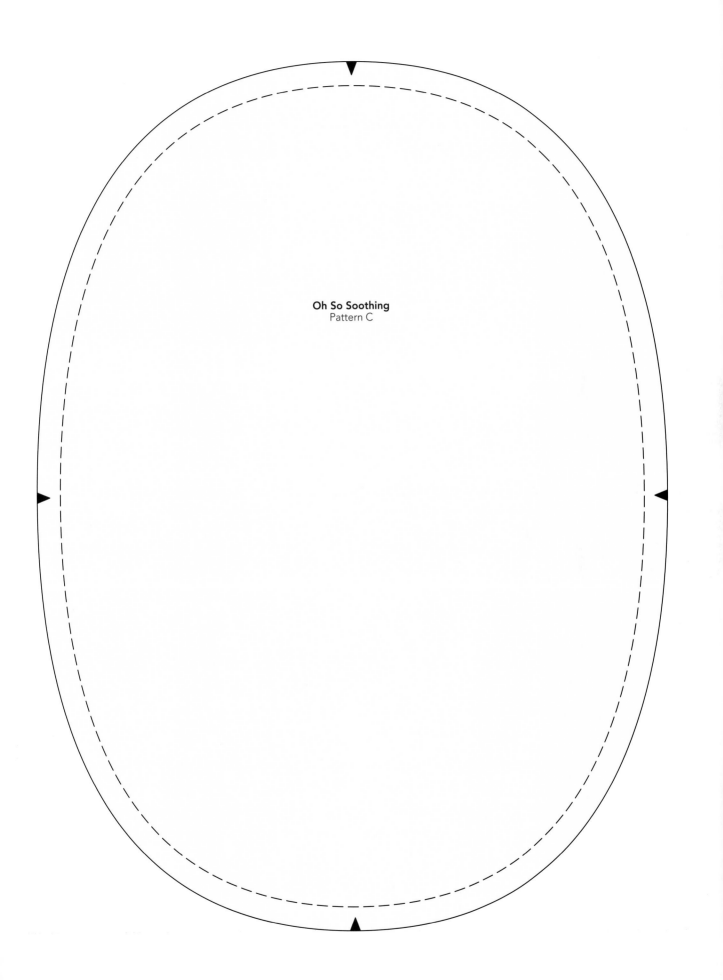

Oh So Soothing
Pattern C

Too many bags? Never!
Not when they're as
easy to sew as this
Four-Patch swing bag.

swing
bag

DESIGNER
TARI COLBY
PHOTOGRAPHER
ADAM ALBRIGHT

materials

- 9×22" piece (fat eighth) black-and-yellow dot (bag)
- 9×22" piece (fat eighth) black-and-yellow circle print (bag)
- ⅓ yard or 18×22" piece (fat quarter) black-and-yellow print (lining)
- ⅓ yard batting
- 2—2" squares fusible interfacing
- 1¾ yards 1"-wide black cotton webbing
- ⅓ yard ½"-diameter black ball fringe trim
- 2—1⅜"-diameter metal rings
- Magnetic snap closure

Finished bag: 9×10"

Quantities are for 44/45"-wide, 100% cotton fabrics.
Measurements include ¼" seam allowances. Sew with right sides together unless otherwise stated.

Perfect for shop hopping, the bag is sized for holding charge cards, cash, keys, swatches, and a cell phone. The long webbing strap allows you to place the bag over your shoulder or across your chest, keeping your hands free to shop.

cut fabrics

Cut pieces in the following order.

From black-and-yellow dot, cut:
- 4—5½×5" rectangles

From black-and-yellow circle print, cut:
- 4—5½×5" rectangles

From black-and-yellow print, cut:
- 1—9½×19" rectangle for lining

From batting, cut:
- 2—9½×10½" rectangles

From webbing, cut:
- 1—1×53" piece
- 2—1×3" pieces

assemble outer bag

1. Referring to **Diagram 1**, lay out two black-and-yellow dot 5½×5" rectangles and two black-and-yellow circle print 5½×5" rectangles in pairs. Join long edges of rectangles in each pair. Press seams in opposite directions. Join pairs to make a Four-Patch unit. Press seam in one direction. The unit should be 9½×10½" including seam allowances. Repeat to make a second Four-Patch unit.

2. Layer a Four-Patch unit and a 9½×10½" batting rectangle; baste together ¼" from outer edges. Repeat with remaining Four-Patch unit and batting rectangle.

3. Referring to **Diagram 2**, align edge of ball fringe trim along one short edge of a Four-Patch unit; baste along basting line.

4. Join Four-Patch units along side and lower edges, being careful not to catch fringe balls in seam (**Diagram 3**). Clip corners; turn right side out and press to make outer bag.

5. Thread one 3"-long webbing piece through one metal ring. Align cut ends of webbing; baste to make a tab. Repeat with remaining 3"-long webbing piece and metal ring.

6. Matching raw edges, position one tab at top left-hand edge of outer bag and the second tab on the opposite side (**Diagram 4**); baste.

DIAGRAM 1

DIAGRAM 2

DIAGRAM 3

DIAGRAM 4

assemble lining

1. Following manufacturer's instructions, center and fuse an interfacing 2″ square to wrong side of black-and-yellow print bag lining ¼″ from short edges **(Diagram 5)**.

2. Attach magnetic snap closure to right side of bag lining ¾″ from short edges **(Diagram 6)**.

¼″

¼″

DIAGRAM 5

¾″

¾″

DIAGRAM 6

DIAGRAM 7

DIAGRAM 8

DIAGRAM 9

3. Fold bag lining in half lengthwise with right sides together. Join side edges, leaving a 4" opening along one side for turning (**Diagram 7**). Clip corners and press to make bag lining.

finish bag

1. Insert outer bag into bag lining right sides together, matching seams; pin. Sew together along top edges (**Diagram 8**).

2. Turn bag to right side through opening in lining. Slip-stitch opening closed. Insert lining into bag; press.

3. Turn under ½" at one end of 53"-long webbing and thread an additional 1½" through one metal ring. Referring to **Diagram 9**, enclose ring and stitch folded edge to secure end of webbing. Repeat with remaining ring and end of webbing on opposite side to make the strap and complete bag.

COLOR OPTION

have a passion for bags?

The Swing Bag is so simple to sew, you can make them by the armload. Change the fabric, change the look. Three of our faves are pictured here (top to bottom): an earthy gold, brown, and blue combination, a modern mix of robin-egg blue and eye-popping red, and a mix of paisleys and florals in brown and lavender hues.

pillows

Soften a chair, a sofa, or a bed with one-of-a-kind pillows. Choose from appliqué pillowcases, striking shams, dimensional toss pillows, and more among the favorites in this collection.

triple play

Choose two kinds of patchwork or a strippy style for punchy pillows to brighten your favorite space.

DESIGNER **PATTY YOUNG**
PHOTOGRAPHER **ADAM ALBRIGHT**

materials for pillow no. 1

- 18×22" piece (fat quarter) each of green geometric, pink geometric, pink floral, and green floral (pillow top, pillow back)

- 2¾ yards green-and-orange-check ruffle trim or 1¼"-wide rickrack

- 2—16½" squares lightweight fusible interfacing

- 16"-square pillow form

Finished pillow: 16" square

materials for pillow no. 2

- 12—3½" squares assorted prints in red, brown, and olive green (pillow top)

- ⅜ yard olive green corduroy (pillow top, pillow back)

- 12½×16½" rectangle lightweight fusible interfacing

- 12×16" pillow form

Finished pillow: 12×16"

materials for pillow no. 3

- ½ yard red stripe (pillow top, pillow back)

- 9×22" piece (fat eighth) brown polka dot (pillow top)

- 5×18" piece each multicolor print and multicolor floral (pillow top)

- 16½" square lightweight fusible interfacing

- 16"-square pillow form

Finished pillow: 16" square

Quantities are for 44/45"-wide, 100% cotton fabrics.
Measurements include ¼" seam allowances. Sew with right sides together unless otherwise stated.

Each of these lively pillows takes just a few pieces of fabric. For best results, fuse lightweight interfacing to the wrong side of each pillow top to add stability and to protect seams from fraying when the pillow cover is washed and dried.

cut fabrics for pillow no. 1

From *each* green geometric, pink geometric, pink floral, and green floral, cut:

- 1—18" square, cutting it diagonally twice in an X for 4 triangles total (you will use 2 of each)

assemble pillow top

1. Referring to **Diagram 1**, lay out one *each* of green and pink geometric, and pink and green floral triangles. Join triangles in pairs; press seams toward floral triangles. Join pairs to make pillow top. Press seams in one direction.

2. Pin and sew ruffle trim or 1¼"-wide rickrack to right side of pillow top along one diagonal seam. Repeat with remaining diagonal seam.

3. Trim pillow top to measure 16½" square including seam allowances.

4. Repeat steps 1–3 to make pillow back.

finish pillow no. 1

1. Following manufacturer's instructions, fuse 16½" interfacing square to wrong side of pillow top and pillow back.

2. Sew pillow front to pillow back, leaving an opening. Turn right side out. Insert pillow form and hand-stitch opening closed.

DIAGRAM 1

editor's tip

Use a chopstick or other blunt object to smoothly round corners of pillow cover when turning it right side out.

cut fabrics for pillow no. 2

Cut pieces in the following order. Cut olive green corduroy lengthwise so that long edges of the rectangles run parallel to the corduroy's wale or ridges.

From olive green corduroy, cut:
- 2—10¾×12½" rectangles
- 2—4×12½" rectangles

assemble pillow top

1. Lay out assorted print 3½" squares in four rows of three squares each (**Diagram 2**). When you are pleased with the arrangement, join squares in each row. Press seams in one direction, alternating direction with each row. Join rows to make pillow top center; press seams in one direction. The pillow top center should be 9½×12½" including seam allowances.

2. Sew olive green corduroy 4×12½" rectangles to long edges of pillow top center to make pillow top (**Diagram 3**). Press seams away from center. The pillow top should be 12½×16½" including seam allowances.

finish pillow no. 2

1. Following manufacturer's instructions, fuse 12½×16½" interfacing rectangle to wrong side of pillow top.

2. Turn under one long edge of each olive green corduroy 10¾×12½" rectangle ¼"; press. Turn under ¼" again and stitch in place to hem pillow back pieces.

3. Referring to **Pillow Back Assembly Diagram**, overlap hemmed edges of pillow back pieces by about 4" to make a 16½×12½" pillow back. Baste overlapped edges.

4. Layer pillow top and back right sides together. Stitch around all edges to make pillow cover.

Turn to right side and press. Insert pillow form through opening in pillow back.

DIAGRAM 2

DIAGRAM 3

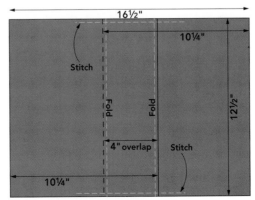

PILLOW BACK ASSEMBLY DIAGRAM

assemble pillow top

Referring to **Diagram 4**, lay out red stripe 4×16½" rectangle and the brown polka dot, multicolor print, and multicolor floral 3⅝×16½" rectangles in a row. Join rectangles to make pillow top; press seams in one direction. The pillow top should be 16½" square including seam allowances.

finish pillow no. 3

1. Following manufacturer's instructions, fuse 16½"interfacing square to wrong side of pillow top.

2. Turn under one long edge of each red stripe 10¾×16½" rectangle ¼"; press. Turn under ¼" again and stitch in place to hem pillow back pieces.

3. Referring to **Pillow Back Assembly Diagram**, overlap hemmed edges of pillow back pieces by about 4" to make a 16½"-square pillow back. Baste overlapped edges.

4. Layer pillow top and back. Stitch around all edges to make pillow cover. Turn to right side and press. Insert pillow form through opening in pillow back.

cut fabrics for pillow no. 3

Cut pieces in the following order.

From red stripe, cut:
- 2—10¾×16½" rectangles
- 1—4×16½" rectangle

From brown polka dot, cut:
- 2—3⅝×16½" rectangles

From *each* multicolor print and multicolor floral, cut:
- 1—3⅝×16½" rectangle

DIAGRAM 4

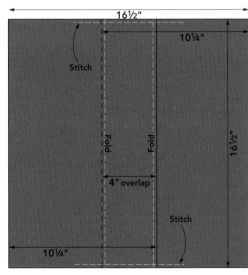

16½"

10¼"

Stitch

Fold

Fold

4" overlap

16½"

Stitch

10¼"

PILLOW BACK ASSEMBLY DIAGRAM

three of a kind

As an alternative, this pillow trio uses a mix of bright pink and green prints. When working with bold prints such as these, audition the prints on a design wall and move them around until you are pleased with the interplay of patterns. If you don't have a design wall, use a piece of cotton flannel on a vertical surface.

wake-up CALL

DESIGNER **DEMETRIA HAYWARD**
PHOTOGRAPHER **GREG SCHEIDEMANN**

Create a zingy, beginner-friendly pillow sham pieced from simple strips. Don't be alarmed by the hand quilting; our step-by-step photos show you how.

materials for one standard-size pillow sham

- ¼ yard solid white (pieced panel)
- ½ yard orange polka dot (pieced panel, binding)
- ¼ yard pink polka dot (pieced panel)
- 1⅛ yards multicolor stripe (pieced panel, pillow back)
- ⅜ yard multicolor dot (border)
- ¾ yard muslin (lining)
- 25×32" batting
- Standard-size bed pillow

Finished pillow sham: 28×21"

Quantities are for 44/45"-wide, 100% cotton fabrics.
Measurements include ¼" seam allowances. Sew with right sides together unless otherwise stated.

When you make one or a pair, this strip-pieced pillow sham is sure to brighten your bed.

cut fabrics

Cut pieces in the following order. Cut multicolor stripe strips and rectangles lengthwise (parallel to the selvages).

From solid white, cut:
- 3—2½×16½" strips
- 2—1½×16½" strips

From orange polka dot, cut:
- 3—4×42" binding strips
- 4—1½×16½" strips

From pink polka dot, cut:
- 4—1¾×16½" strips

From multicolor stripe, cut:
- 2—18×21" rectangles
- 4—2×16½" strips

From multicolor dot, cut:
- 2—2¾×28" border strips
- 2—2¾×16½" border strips

From muslin, cut:
- 1—25×32" rectangle

interlocking circles across the pillow sham top (see Big-Stitch Quilting, *opposite*).

3. Trim quilted pillow sham top to 28×21" including seam allowances.

finish pillow sham

1. Turn under 1" along one 21" edge of each multicolor stripe 18×21" rectangle; press. Turn under 1" again and stitch in place to hem pillow back pieces.

2. Referring to **Pillow Sham Back Assembly Diagram**, overlap hemmed edges of pillow back pieces by about 4" to make a 28×21" pillow sham back. Baste overlapped edges.

3. Layer pillow sham top and back wrong sides together. Baste around all edges. Using ½" seam allowance, bind with orange polka dot binding strips to complete pillow sham. (For details, see Better Binding, *page 160*.) Insert pillow.

assemble pillow sham top

1. Referring to **Pillow Sham Assembly Diagram**, lay out solid white 1½×16½" strips, orange polka dot 1½×16½" strips, pink polka dot 1¾×16½" strips, multicolor stripe 2×16½" strips, and solid white 2½×16½" strips in a row. Join strips to make pillow sham center panel; press seams in one direction. The pillow sham center panel should be 23½×16½" including seam allowances.

2. Add short multicolor dot border strips to short edges of pillow sham center panel. Join long multicolor dot border strips to long edges to make pillow sham top. Press seams toward border.

quilt pillow sham top

1. Layer pillow sham top, batting, and muslin; baste. (For details, see Complete the Quilt, *page 160*.)

2. Quilt as desired. Project maker Rhoda Nelson hand-quilted

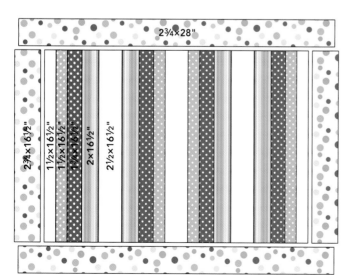

2¾×28"

2¾×16½" 1½×16½" 1½×16½" 1¾×16½" 2×16½" 2½×16½"

PILLOW SHAM ASSEMBLY DIAGRAM

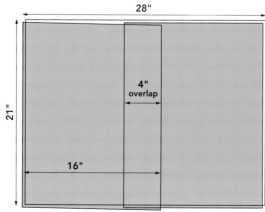

28"

4" overlap

21"

16"

PILLOW SHAM BACK ASSEMBLY DIAGRAM

tropical mix

Pay token to your island wanderlust with this version of Wake-Up Call made of jewel-tone batiks. In-the-ditch quilting complements the richly patterned fabrics.

big-stitch quilting

Also known as utility quilting, big-stitch quilting is a quick, simple hand-quilting technique that results in a primitive, folk art look. Here's how to create this look using assorted dinner plates and drinking glasses as quilting guides.

1. Tape pillow sham top to flat surface. Use water-soluble marker to draw around largest plate to mark circle pattern on fabric for quilting guide (**Photo 1**).
2. Center a smaller plate inside larger circle and mark as before (**Photo 2**). Continue adding assorted sizes of circles as desired.
3. Layer the pillow sham top, batting, and muslin; baste.
4. Use quilting-weight thread, a sharp needle, and a long hand stitch (three to four running stitches per inch) to quilt layers together (**Photo 3**).

PHOTO 1   PHOTO 2   PHOTO 3

POP ART

DESIGNERS **LAURA GUNN**
AND PATTI PINKSTON
PHOTOGRAPHER **GREG**
SCHEIDEMANN

Shapely appliqué, feminine fringe, and ruffled rosettes—this bedecked beauty turns heads with just the right accessories.

materials

- ½ yard blue-and-yellow print (appliqués)
- ¼ yard wine red print (appliqués)
- ¾ yard lime green print (pillow front/appliqué foundation)
- 1⅜ yards aqua polka dot (pillow back, rosettes)
- 2 yards ball fringe: purple
- Thread: purple
- Fusible web
- 18"-square pillow form
- Polyester fiberfill

Finished pillow: 18" square

Quantities are for 44/45"-wide, 100% cotton fabrics.
Measurements include ½" seam allowances unless otherwise stated. Sew with right sides together unless otherwise stated.

cut fabrics

Cut pieces in the following order. Patterns are on *Pattern Sheet 1*.

To use fusible web for appliquéing, complete the following steps. (For more information on fusible appliqué, see Piece and Appliqué, *page 158*.)

1. Lay fusible web, paper side up, over Pattern C. Use a pencil to trace the pattern six times.

2. Cut out fusible-web shapes on drawn lines. Do not remove paper backings.

From blue-and-yellow print, cut:
- 12 of Pattern A

From wine red print, cut:
- 12 of Pattern B

From lime green print, cut:
- 1—19" square

From aqua polka dot, cut:
- 3—2×40" strips
- 2—23×19" rectangles

appliqué pillow top

1. With right sides together, join two blue-and-yellow print A pieces using a ¼" seam (**Diagram 1**). Trim seam allowances.

2. Gently pull fabric layers apart and snip a small slash through one layer of fabric. Keeping fabric layers separate, enlarge slash to make a 2"-long slit in one layer (**Diagram 2**).

DIAGRAM 1

DIAGRAM 2

3. Turn joined A pieces to right side through slit in fabric to make a large petal. Press.

4. Following manufacturer's instructions, press a fusible-web C piece onto back side (with slit) of large petal. Peel off paper backing.

5. Repeat steps 1–4 to make six large petals total.

6. Using two wine red print B pieces, repeat steps 1–3 to make a small petal.

7. Insert a small amount of fiberfill through slit in back side of small petal. Whipstitch opening closed.

8. Repeat steps 6 and 7 to make six small petals total.

9. Referring to **Appliqué Placement Diagram**, arrange large petals on lime green print 19" square. Fuse pieces in place and machine-blanket-stitch with purple thread.

assemble pillow cover

1. Aligning woven edge of ball fringe with edges of pillow top, baste ball fringe in place (**Diagram 3**).

2. With wrong sides inside, fold each aqua polka dot 23×19" rectangle in half to form two double-thick 11½×19" pieces. (The double thickness makes the pillow back more stable.) Overlap folded edges by about 4" to make a 19" square (**Diagram 4**). Stitch across overlapped edges to make pillow back.

3. With right sides together, layer pillow top with pillow back. Using a ½" seam, sew around outer edges to make pillow cover, being careful to catch only the header on the ball fringe in the seam allowance. Turn pillow cover right side out; press.

assemble and add rosettes

1. With wrong side inside, fold and press an aqua polka dot 2×40" strip in half lengthwise to make a 1"-wide strip.

2. With a long machine-basting stitch, sew ¼" from raw edges of 1"-wide strip. Pull threads to gather strip to make a 17"-long ruffle (**Diagram 5**).

3. Fold one end of gathered strip at a 45-degree angle, aligning strip end with long raw edge of strip (**Diagram 6**). Using needle and thread, tack fabric fold in place near gathering stitches.

4. Working with gathered strip, make a small half-fold over previously tacked fabric and tack again to make rosette center. Continue wrapping gathered strip around center, tacking at each turn. When close to end, fold strip end at 45-degree angle and stitch in place to finish rosette.

5. Repeat steps 1–4 to make three rosettes total.

6. Referring to photo on *page 76* for placement, hand-stitch rosettes at pillow center. Insert pillow form to complete pillow.

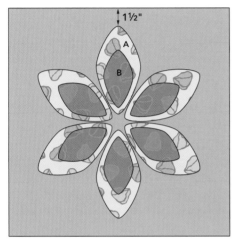

APPLIQUÉ PLACEMENT DIAGRAM

DIAGRAM 3

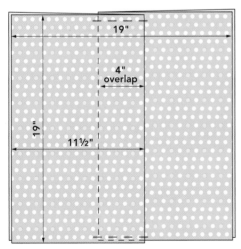

DIAGRAM 4

DIAGRAM 5

DIAGRAM 6

straight &
narrow

Fabric scraps take center stage on a pair of geometric pillows.

DESIGNERS **JEAN AND VALORI WELLS**
PHOTOGRAPHER **CAMERON SADEGHPOUR**

materials

- ¼ yard muslin (piecing foundations)
- ¼ yard solid light green (pieced panels, border)
- ¼ yard solid light turquoise (pieced panels, corner triangles)
- ⅞ yard green floral (pieced panels, borders, pillow backs)
- ⅛ yard *each* solid dark green, solid dark turquoise, and solid yellow (pieced panels)
- Polyester fiberfill

Finished pillows: 12" square and 12×22"

Quantities are for 44/45"-wide, 100% cotton fabrics.
Measurements include ¼" seam allowances. Sew with right sides together unless otherwise stated.

Dig into the bits and pieces of your fabric stash to strip-piece the center panels for each of these striking pillows. All you need are twelve different pieces that are at least 6" long.

cut fabrics

Cut pieces in the following order.

From muslin, cut:
- 1—5×16" piecing foundation
- 1—6"-square piecing foundation

From solid light green, cut:
- 2—2½×18½" border strips
- 2—2½×4½" border strips

From solid light turquoise, cut:
- 2—5" squares, cutting each in half diagonally for 4 corner triangles total

From green floral, cut:
- 1—12½×22½" pillow back
- 2—2½×22½" border strips
- 1—12½"-square pillow back
- 2—2½×12½" border strips
- 4—2½×8½" border strips

From solid dark green, solid dark turquoise, solid yellow, and the scraps of solid light green, solid light turquoise, and green floral, cut:
- 12—6"-long strips in widths ranging from ¾" to 1½"
- 25—5"-long strips in widths ranging from ¾" to 1½"

assemble pieced panels

1. With right side up, align an assorted solid or floral 6"-long strip with an edge of muslin 6" square. With right side down, place a second assorted strip atop first strip. Sew together through all layers (**Diagram 1**). Finger-press top strip open (**Diagram 2**). Continue adding assorted solid and floral strips until muslin square is covered; press. Trim covered muslin square to 5¾" square including seam allowances to make square pieced panel.

2. Referring to Step 1, cover muslin 5×16" rectangle with assorted solid and floral 5"-long strips. Trim to 4½×14½" including seam allowances to make rectangular pieced panel.

DIAGRAM 1   DIAGRAM 2

assemble pillows

1. Sew solid light turquoise corner triangles to opposite edges of square pieced panel (**Diagram 3**). Add solid light turquoise corner triangles to remaining edges; press all seams toward triangles. Trim to 8½" square including seam allowances to make square pillow center.

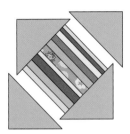

DIAGRAM 3

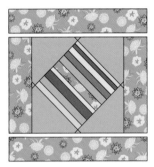

DIAGRAM 4

Whenever you finish a project, cut your remaining fabric into assorted-width strips and store them in see-through plastic bags that are clearly marked with the strip width. Over time, you'll collect an assortment that you can turn into a scrappy quilt or interesting pillow centers!

2. Add green floral 2½×8½" border strips to opposite edges of square pillow center. Add green floral 2½×12½" border strips to remaining edges to complete square pillow top (**Diagram 4**). Press all seams toward border. The pillow top should be 12½" square including seam allowances.

3. Join solid light green 2½×4½" border strips to short edges of rectangular pieced panel. Add solid light green 2½×18½" border strips to remaining edges; press all seams toward border. Sew green floral 2½×8½" border strips to short edges of pillow center. Add green floral 2½×22½" border strips to remaining edges to complete rectangular pillow top. Press all seams toward green floral border. The pillow top should be 12½×22½" including seam allowances.

4. Sew each pillow front to its corresponding-size green floral pillow back, leaving an opening. Turn right sides out. Stuff with fiberfill and hand-stitch openings closed.

editor's tip

A quick stitch-and-flip method brings together narrow fabric strips to create the striped centers on these pillows. Choose a different fabric for the back, and you can create a reversible pillow that offers a new look.

Flash back to the '60s—the days of peace, love, and rock 'n' roll—while lounging on a floor-size pillow stitched from retro prints.

peace out

DESIGNER **KELLY ALFORD**
PHOTOGRAPHER **GREG SCHEIDEMANN**

materials for one floor pillow

- ⅝ yard brown floral (appliqué)
- 1⅞ yards multicolor print (appliqué foundation, pillow back)
- ⅝ yard solid fuchsia (appliqué)
- 1¼ yards peace symbol print (border)
- 1¼ yards lightweight fusible web
- 40" square backing fabric
- 40" square batting

- 1×27" strip hook-and-loop tape
- 30"-square pillow form
- Monofilament thread (optional)

Finished pillow: 37" square

Quantities are for 44/45"-wide, 100% cotton fabrics.
Measurements include ½" seam allowances. Sew with right sides together unless otherwise stated.

cut fabrics

Cut pieces in the following order. The patterns are on *Pattern Sheet 2*.

To use fusible web for appliquéing, complete the following steps. (For more information on fusible appliqué, see Piece and Appliqué, *page 158*.)

1. Lay fusible web, paper side up, over patterns. Use a pencil to trace each pattern once, leaving ½" between tracings. Cut out each fusible-web shape roughly ¼" outside traced lines.

2. Following manufacturer's instructions, press fusible-web shapes onto wrong sides of designated fabrics; let cool. Cut out fabric shapes on drawn lines. Peel off paper backings.

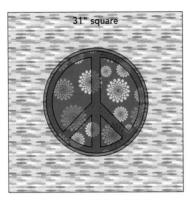

APPLIQUÉ PLACEMENT DIAGRAM

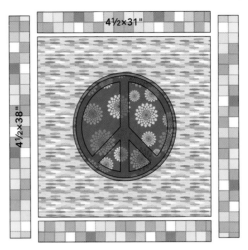

PILLOW TOP ASSEMBLY DIAGRAM

From brown floral, cut:
- 1 of Pattern A

From multicolor print, cut:
- 1—31" square
- 2—19½×31" rectangles

From solid fuchsia, cut:
- 1 of Pattern B

From peace symbol print, cut:
- 4—4½×38" border strips
- 4—4½×31" border strips

assemble and appliqué pillow top

1. Referring to **Appliqué Placement Diagram**, center brown floral A circle on multicolor print 31" square. Fuse in place.

2. Center solid fuchsia B shape over fused circle (solid fuchsia B shape is larger than fused circle); fuse in place.

3. Referring to **Pillow Top Assembly Diagram**, sew short border strips to opposite edges of pillow center. Press seams open. Add long border strips to remaining edges to make pillow top. Press seams open. The pillow top should be 38" square including seam allowances.

4. Layer pillow top, batting, and backing; baste. (For details, see Complete the Quilt, *page 160*.)

5. Using matching thread or monofilament thread, machine-appliqué around appliqué shapes through all layers.

6. With appliqué centered, trim pillow top to be 38" square including seam allowances.

finish pillow

1. Turn under one long edge of each multicolor print 19½×31" rectangle 1"; press. Turn under 1" again and stitch in place to hem pillow back pieces.

2. Center and sew one part of hook-and-loop tape to hemmed edge on wrong side of one pillow back piece (**Diagram 1**; note placement of tape from hemmed edge). Repeat, sewing other part of hook-and-loop tape to right side of remaining pillow back piece, 14" from unhemmed edge; again note placement of tape.

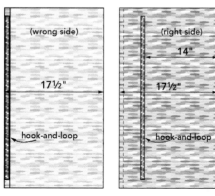

DIAGRAM 1

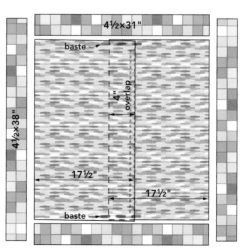

PILLOW BACK ASSEMBLY DIAGRAM

3. Referring to **Pillow Back Assembly Diagram**, overlap hemmed edges of pillow back pieces by about 4" to make a 31"-square pillow back center. Baste overlapped edges.

4. Referring to Assemble and Appliqué Pillow Top, Step 3, *page 85*, join border strips to pillow back center to make pillow back.

5. Layer pillow top and pillow back right sides together. Stitch around all edges. Turn to right side and press.

6. Align pillow front and pillow back border seams. Referring to **Diagram 2**, stitch in the ditch around all sides between pillow center and border to complete pillow cover. Insert pillow form through opening.

stitch in the ditch

DIAGRAM 2

editor's tip

You can rotary-cut several layers of fabric simultaneously. For best results, rotary-cut no more than four thicknesses at a time.

COLOR OPTION

butterflies galore

Four printed panels make up the center block of this floor pillow. This pillow top features black dot flat piping added to the center, and a border of printed butterflies.

Contrasting fabrics, eye-catching appliqués, and frayed edges create visual and textural appeal in this pillow. You'll quilt the pillow top before creating the ragged-edge look.

spot ON!

DESIGNER
JENNI PAIGE
PHOTOGRAPHER
KRITSADA

materials

- Large scraps of assorted cream batiks and prints (blocks)
- Scraps of black batiks (appliqués)
- 20" square muslin (lining)
- 17" square backing fabric
- 20" square lightweight batting
- Quilt basting spray
- 16"-square pillow form

Finished pillow: 16" square
Finished block: 8" square

Quantities are for 44/45"-wide, 100% cotton fabrics.
Measurements include ½" seam allowances. Sew with wrong sides together unless otherwise stated.

- - - - - - - - - - - - - - - - - -

The frayed edges on this pillow may appear to be the result of wear-and-tear, but they're intentionally put there with snips taken in the exposed seam allowances. The key to the look is to sew the pieces together with wrong sides together.

cut fabrics

Cut pieces in the following order. The Circle Pattern is on *Pattern Sheet 1.* To make a template of the pattern, see Make and Use Templates, *page 158.*

From assorted cream batiks and prints, cut:
- 4—3×9" rectangles for position 4
- 8—3×7" rectangles for positions 2 and 3
- 4—3×5" rectangles for position 1
- 4—5" squares

From black batiks, cut:
- 2 of Circle Pattern

assemble blocks

Note: Sew using ½" seam allowances. All seams are sewn with wrong sides together, 10 to 14 stitches per inch.

1. Sew together a cream batik or print 5" square and a position 1 rectangle (**Diagram 1**). Press seam toward position 1 rectangle.

2. Referring to **Diagram 2**, add a cream batik or print position 2 rectangle to top edge of pieced Step 1 unit. Press seam toward added rectangle.

3. Referring to **Diagram 3**, add a cream batik or print position 3 rectangle to right side of pieced Step 2 unit. Press seam as before.

4. Referring to **Diagram 4**, add a cream batik or print position 4 rectangle to top of pieced Step 3 unit to make a block. Press seam as before. The block should be 9" square including seam allowances.

5. Repeat steps 1–4 to make four blocks total.

assemble pillow

1. Referring to photo *opposite,* lay out blocks in pairs. Sew together blocks in each pair; press seams in opposite directions. Join pairs to make pillow top. The pillow top should be 17" square including seam allowances. Place a black batik circle on two cream batik or print squares; baste in place.

2. Layer pillow top, batting, and muslin lining. (For details, see Complete the Quilt, *page 160.*)

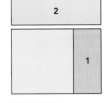

DIAGRAM 1   **DIAGRAM 2**

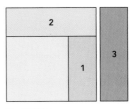

DIAGRAM 3

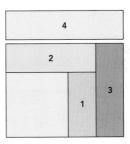

DIAGRAM 4

3. Quilt as desired (be careful not to catch seam allowances so they can be clipped later). A spiral design is machine-quilted in each appliqué; parallel lines are stitched elsewhere.

4. Trim lining and batting even with pillow top edges. Machine-baste layers of pillow top ⅜" from outside edges.

5. To fray pillow top raw edges, make ¼"-deep cuts ½" apart in the seams. Then machine-wash the pillow top in a warm-water-wash and cool-rinse cycle with a small amount of detergent; machine-dry.

6. With right sides together, layer pillow top and 17" square backing; pin. Sew together, leaving an opening for pillow form. Turn right side out and insert pillow form; slip-stitch opening closed.

P IS FOR pillow

Get practice piecing triangles while you make this oversized child's pillow from 1930s prints.

PROJECT MAKER **KAREN GILSON**
PHOTOGRAPHER **CAMERON SADEGHPOUR**

materials

- ¼ yard blue print (blocks)
- ¼ yard yellow polka dot (blocks)
- 2 yards red print (blocks, outer border, pillow back)
- ¼ yard green polka dot (blocks)
- ⅜ yard blue polka dot (inner border, binding)
- 30" square muslin (lining)
- 30" square batting
- 24"-square pillow form

Finished Pillow: 24" square
Finished Block: 8" square

Quantities are for 44/45"-wide, 100% cotton fabrics.
Measurements include ¼" seam allowances. Sew with right sides together unless otherwise stated.

Playful novelty prints and polka dots in primary colors make this oversized pillow a fun addition to a child's bedroom or family game room. Two borders frame the four-block pillow center, easily pieced with two sizes of triangles, to make an ample 24"-square floor cushion ideal for playing games or watching television. We think you'll discover that one pillow isn't enough, but with a project this simple, you can stitch enough for everyone in the family!

cut fabrics

Cut pieces in the following order.

From blue print, cut:
- 1—6⅞" square, cutting it in half diagonally for 2 large triangles total
- 7—2⅞" squares, cutting each in half diagonally for 14 small triangles total

From yellow polka dot, cut:
- 1—6⅞" square, cutting it in half diagonally for 2 large triangles total
- 7—2⅞" squares, cutting each in half diagonally for 14 small triangles total

From red print, cut:
- 2—24½×30½" rectangles
- 2—3½×24½" outer border strips
- 2—3½×18½" outer border strips
- 1—6⅞" square, cutting it in half diagonally for 2 large triangles total
- 7—2⅞" squares, cutting each in half diagonally for 14 small triangles total

From green polka dot, cut:
- 1—6⅞" square, cutting it in half diagonally for 2 large triangles total
- 7—2⅞" squares, cutting each in half diagonally for 14 small triangles total

From blue polka dot, cut:
- 3—2½×42" binding strips
- 2—1½×18½" inner border strips
- 2—1½×16½" inner border strips

assemble blocks

1. Sew together a blue print small triangle and a yellow polka dot small triangle to make a triangle-square (**Diagram 1**). Press seam toward blue print. The triangle-square should be 2½" square including seam allowances. Repeat to make four triangle-squares total.

2. Referring to **Diagram 2**, lay out triangle-squares, three blue print small triangles, and three yellow polka dot small triangles in sections. Sew together pieces in each section; press seams toward triangles. Join sections to make a center unit; press seams in one direction.

3. Join a blue print large triangle and a yellow polka dot large triangle to long edges of center unit to make a blue-and-yellow block (**Diagram 3**). Press seams toward large triangles. The block should be 8½" square including seam allowances.

4. Repeat steps 1 through 3 to make a second blue-and-yellow block.

5. Repeat steps 1 through 3 using red print and green polka dot large and small triangles to make two red-and-green blocks.

assemble pillow center

1. Referring to **Pillow Assembly Diagram**, lay out blocks in pairs. Sew together pairs; press seams in opposite directions.

2. Join pairs to make pillow center. Press seam in one direction. The pillow center should be 16½" square including seam allowances.

add borders

1. Sew short blue polka dot inner border strips to opposite edges of pillow center. Add long blue polka dot inner border strips to remaining edges. Press seams toward inner border.

2. Join short red print outer border strips to opposite edges of pillow center. Add long red print outer border strips to remaining edges to complete pillow top. Press seams toward outer border.

finish pillow

1. Layer pillow top, batting, and muslin lining; baste. (For details, see Complete the Quilt, *page 160*.) Quilt as desired.

2. With wrong side inside, fold each red print 24½×30½" rectangle in half to make two 24½×15¼" double-thick pillow back rectangles. Referring to **Diagram 4**, overlap folded edges of pillow back rectangles by 6" to make a 24½"-square pillow back. Baste ¼" from top and bottom edges to secure pieces.

3. With wrong sides together, layer pillow top and pillow back. Sew together along all edges to make pillow cover.

4. Bind with blue polka dot binding strips. (For details, see Better Binding, *page 160*.) Insert pillow form through opening in pillow back.

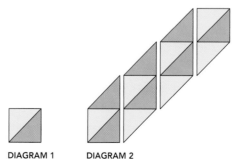

DIAGRAM 1   DIAGRAM 2

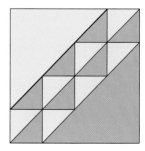

DIAGRAM 3

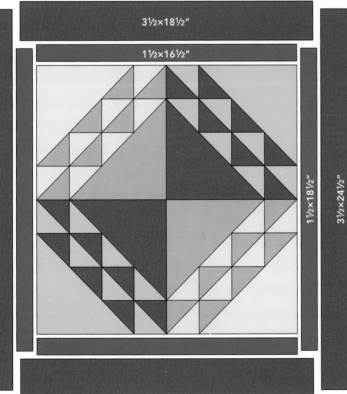

3½×18½"

1½×16½"

1½×18½"

3½×24½"

PILLOW ASSEMBLY DIAGRAM

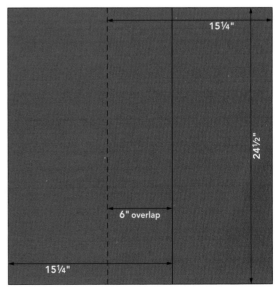

15¼"

24½"

6" overlap

15¼"

DIAGRAM 4

KNOT worthy

DESIGNER **JOANIE HOLTON**
PHOTOGRAPHER
CAMERON SADEGHPOUR

Surprisingly small, this pillow packs a punch. Make several and toss them on a chair to add color and drama.

materials

- ¼ yard purple-and-black print (pillow, piping, covered cording, covered button)
- ⅜ yard purple-and-white print (pillow, covered cording)
- 20"-long ¼"-diameter cording
- ¾"-diameter button to cover
- 12"-square pillow form
- Dollmaker's needle
- Heavy-duty thread
- Small safety pin

Finished pillow: 12" square

Quantities are for 44/45"-wide, 100% cotton fabrics.
Measurements include ¼" seam allowances. Sew with right sides together unless otherwise stated.

It's only a Four-Patch framed with flat piping, but the cord-filled Japanese knot adds a decorator's touch to this sassy pillow. Our easy-to-follow instructions will show you exactly how to add the piping and weave the attractive knot.

cut fabrics

Cut pieces in the following order.

From purple-and-black print, cut:

- 2—¾×42" strips for piping
- 2—6½" squares
- Enough 1¼"-wide bias strips to total 12" for cording (See Cutting on the Bias on *page 159.*)
- 1—2" square

From purple-and-white print, cut:

- 1—12½" square
- 2—6½" squares
- Enough 1¼"-wide bias strips to total 12" for cording

assemble pillow top

1. Using a diagonal seam, sew together purple-and-black print ¾×42" strips to make an 83½"-long pieced strip.

2. With wrong side inside, fold pieced strip in half lengthwise; press. Cut to make:
   - 1—50" piping strip
   - 1—12½" piping strip
   - 2—6½" piping strips

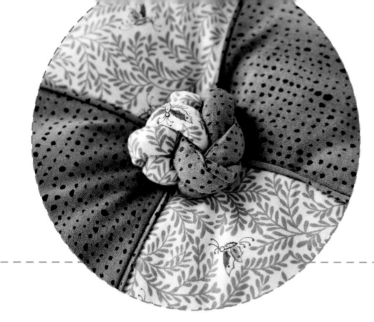

3. Aligning raw edges and with right sides together, sew a 6½" piping strip to one edge of a purple-and-black print 6½" square (Diagram 1). Repeat with remaining 6½" piping strip and purple-and-black print 6½" square.

4. Join each Step 3 purple-and-black print 6½" square with a purple-and-white print 6½" square along piped edge to make a block unit (Diagram 2). Repeat to make a second block unit. Press all seams toward purple-and-black print squares.

5. Aligning raw edges as before, sew 12½" piping strip to one edge of a block unit.

6. Sew together piped block unit and remaining block unit along piped edge to make a Four-Patch (Diagram 3). Press seam to one side.

7. Open one end of 50" folded piping strip. Fold end under 1½"; finger-press. Refold strip in half lengthwise.

8. Aligning raw edges and using a scant ¼" seam, baste piping to all edges of Four-Patch, starting 1½" from folded end. As you stitch each corner, clip seam allowance to within a few threads of basting line (Diagram 4); gently ease piping in place. Insert free end of piping into folded end, and baste to beginning point to complete pillow top.

assemble pillow

Layer pillow top and purple-and-white print 12½" square. Sew together along all edges, leaving an opening along one side for turning. Turn right side out. Insert pillow form through opening; hand-stitch opening closed.

assemble and add decorative knot

1. Aligning short edges, sew together purple-and-black print bias strips to make a 10"-long pieced strip.

2. Fold pieced strip in half lengthwise, right side inside. Sew together along long edge. Attach a small safety pin to one end of strip. Work safety pin through channel to turn strip right side out and make a tube; press.

3. Cut cording into two 10" lengths. Attach a safety pin to one end of a cording piece and work through tube to make purple-and-black covered cording.

4. Repeat steps 1–3 with purple-and-white print bias strips and remaining 10"-long cording piece to make purple-and-white covered cording.

5. Referring to Diagram 5, lay out purple-and-black and purple-and-white cording. Weave cording pieces together as shown, pulling cording pieces taut, to make knot.

6. Turn knot to back side. Trim purple-and-black cording ends to within 1" of knot. Remove 1" of stitching at each end of cording and pull back bias strip ends. Trim cording so ends abut and whipstitch them together (Diagram 6). Refold bias strip so it covers cording, turning top strip under ½". Hand-stitch strip to close seam and cover cording.

7. Repeat Step 6 with purple-and-white cording.

8. Following manufacturer's instructions, cover button with purple-and-black print 2" square.

9. Thread and knot dollmaker's needle with heavy-duty thread. Stitch down through center of pillow to back side and attach covered button. Stitch back up to pillow top. Taking small stitches through knot and pillow top, secure knot firmly in place.

editor's tip

To quickly insert a pillow form into a pillow cover,
place form in a plastic bag, which helps it slide into the cover.
Remove plastic bag before stitching the opening closed.

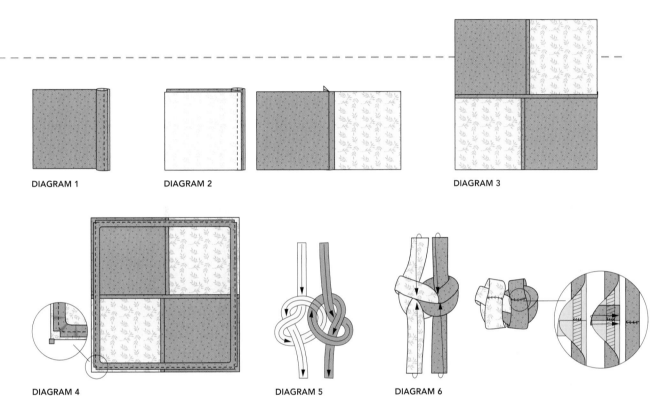

DIAGRAM 1

DIAGRAM 2

DIAGRAM 3

DIAGRAM 4

DIAGRAM 5

DIAGRAM 6

COLOR OPTION

velvety smooth

Step out of the quilter's comfort zone and give glamour fabric a try on a small project such as Knot Worthy. Orange and dark red velveteen pair up in this striking version. If you use velveteen, just remember, velveteen is a directional fabric, so plan to cut all pieces with the nap running in the same direction. Press velveteen on reverse side, using spray starch or sizing to help stabilize the fabric and minimize fraying. Sew with a new, sharp needle, size 70 or 80, and 100% cotton thread.

DESIGNER **LESLEY MEHMEN**
PHOTOGRAPHER **ADAM ALBRIGHT**

gather 'round

Learn two great ways to make yo-yos
for this sweet little accent pillow.

materials

- 40—5" squares assorted prints
  (yo-yos, pillow back)

- ⅓ yard muslin (pillow top, lining)

- 2—9½" squares batting

- Polyester fiberfill

- Clover Quick Yo-Yo Maker, size
  large (optional)

Finished pillow: 9" square

Quantities are for 44/45"-wide,
100% cotton fabrics.
Measurements include ¼" seam
allowances. Sew with right sides
together unless otherwise stated.

*Once you learn how to make
yo-yos, you'll find it hard to stop!
Whip up a handful, then join them
together in rows to make this
miniature pillow.*

cut fabrics

Cut pieces in the following order.
The Circle Pattern is on *page 101*.
To make a template of the
Circle Pattern, see Make and
Use Templates on *page 158*.

From assorted prints, cut:
- 36 of Circle Pattern (If using
  Yo-Yo Maker, see directions for
  cutting under Assemble Yo-Yos:
  Method 2, *page 100*.)

From muslin, cut:
- 3—9½" squares

assemble yo-yos: method 1

Thread a needle with matching or
neutral thread and tie a knot about
6" from end. With an assorted print
circle facedown, turn raw edge
of circle a scant ¼" toward circle
center. Take small, evenly spaced
running stitches (**Running Stitch
Diagram** on *page 136*) near the
folded edge to secure it (**Photo 1**).
End stitching next to the starting
point. Do not cut thread. Gently
pull thread ends to gather folded
edge until it forms a gathered circle
(**Photo 2**). Knot and trim thread
to make a yo-yo. Repeat to make
36 yo-yos total.

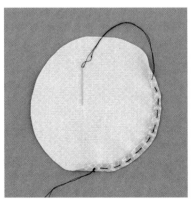

PHOTO 1

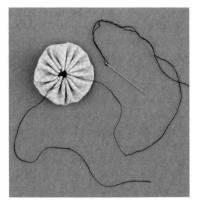

PHOTO 2

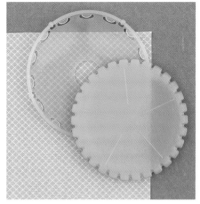

PHOTO 3

PHOTO 4

PHOTO 5

assemble yo-yos: method 2

1. Layer the Yo-Yo Maker disk (**Photo 3**), right side up, atop wrong side of an assorted print 5" square. (The disk's right side is the side with printing.) Insert disk and print square into plate, aligning disk lines with protrusions on plate. Press firmly to secure disk, fabric, and plate together (**Photo 4**).

2. Leaving about ³⁄₁₆" from edge of plate for seam allowance, cut away excess fabric (**Photo 5**).

3. Thread a short needle with matching thread, and tie a knot about 6" from end. Fold seam allowance in toward disk center and hold in place. Insert needle into concave part of disk beneath seam allowance and pull out through hole in plate (**Photo 6**).

4. With plate side up, continue to hold seam allowance down and work counterclockwise, pushing needle down through next hole, then up through following hole. Repeat to make running stitches around circle, going one hole beyond starting point and pulling needle out through disk side (**Photo 7**).

5. Remove disk from plate. Gently lift seam allowance and remove disk from fabric circle. Pull thread ends to gather circle into a yo-yo; knot thread ends and trim.

6. Repeat steps 1–5 to make 36 yo-yos total.

assemble pillow cover

1. Referring to **Pillow Back Assembly Diagram**, join remaining four assorted print 5" squares in pairs. Press seams in opposite directions. Join pairs to make pillow back.

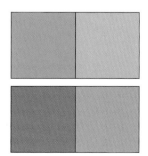

PILLOW BACK ASSEMBLY DIAGRAM

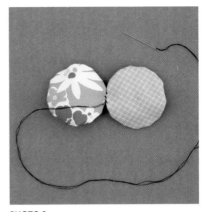

PHOTO 6   PHOTO 7   PHOTO 8

Press seams in one direction. The pillow back should be 9½" square including seam allowances.

2. Layer pillow back, a batting 9½" square, and a muslin 9½" square; baste. Quilt as desired. (For details, see Complete the Quilt, *page 160*.) Lesley machine-quilted the pillow back in a 1" diagonal grid. In the same manner, layer and quilt remaining two muslin squares and batting square to make quilted pillow top.

3. With right sides together, sew quilted pillow top to quilted pillow back to make pillow cover, leaving a 3" opening along one edge for turning. Turn pillow cover right side out. Stuff with fiberfill through opening. Whipstitch opening closed.

finish pillow

1. Lay out yo-yos in six rows. When pleased with the arrangement, place yo-yos with gathered fronts together and whipstitch to join, stitching about ½" (**Photo 8**). Join rows in same manner to make yo-yo square.

2. Referring to photograph, *opposite*, center and pin yo-yo square to quilted pillow top. Whipstitch outer edges of yo-yo square to pillow top seam lines to complete pillow.

editor's tip

Double your thread when making yo-yos. When you pull on the thread to gather the center, the double thread is less likely to break.

Gather 'Round
Circle Pattern

Make a sophisticated style
statement on a budget with
classic accent pillows.

three's
COMPANY

DESIGNER **LYNETTE JENSEN**
PHOTOGRAPHERS **GREG SCHEIDEMANN AND MARTY BALDWIN**

patchwork pillow
materials

- ¼ yard red dot (pillow top)

- ¼ yard gold print (pillow top)

- ¼ yard green print (pillow top)

- 1 yard multicolor floral
  (pillow top and back)

- ¼ yard green stripe (binding)

- 21" square muslin (lining)

- 21" square batting

- 18"-square pillow form

Finished pillow: 18" square

Quantities are for 44/45"-wide,
100% cotton fabrics.
Measurements include
¼" seam allowances unless
otherwise stated. Sew with
right sides together unless
otherwise stated.

*Deceptively simple in design,
these three accent pillows are
great projects for beginning
quilters. One uses patchwork,
another strip piecing; the third
combines patchwork and
appliqué. Experiment using
different appliqué shapes for
your own unique look.*

cut and assemble patchwork pillow

Cut pieces in the following order.

From red dot, cut:
- 2—6¾×8¾" rectangles

From gold print, cut:
- 2—4¾×6½" rectangles
- 2—2½×6¾" rectangles

From green print, cut:
- 2—6¾×8¾" rectangles

From multicolor floral, cut:
- 2—19×23" rectangles
- 1—6½×10½" rectangle

From green stripe, cut:
- 2—3×42" binding strips

1. Referring to **Patchwork Pillow Assembly Diagram**, lay out rectangles in three rows. Sew together pieces in each row. Press seams in one direction, alternating direction with each row. Join rows to make pillow top. Press seams in one direction.

2. Layer pillow top with batting and muslin lining; baste. (For details, see Complete the Quilt, *page 160*.) Quilt as desired. Trim batting and lining even with pillow top edges.

3. With wrong side inside, fold each multicolor floral 19×23" rectangle in half to form two double-thick 19×11½" rectangles. (The double thickness makes the pillow back more stable.) Overlap folded edges of double-thick rectangles by about 4" to make a 19" square (**Pillow Back Assembly Diagram**). Baste ½" from edges to make pillow back.

4. Layer pillow top and back wrong sides together; join with ½" seam. Bind with green stripe binding strips using ½" seams. (For details, see Better Binding, *page 160*.) Insert pillow form through opening.

stripe pillow
materials

- ¼ yard green stripe (pillow top)
- ⅛ yard dark red print (pillow top)
- ⅔ yard red dot (pillow top and back)
- 19" square muslin (lining)
- 19" square batting
- 16"-square pillow form

Finished pillow: 16" square

Quantities are for 44/45"-wide, 100% cotton fabrics. **Measurements** include ¼" seam allowances. Sew with right sides together unless otherwise stated.

cut and assemble stripe pillow

Cut pieces in the following order.

From green stripe, cut:
- 2—4½×16½" rectangles

PATCHWORK PILLOW ASSEMBLY DIAGRAM

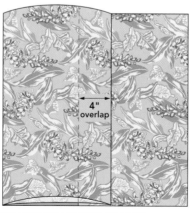

PILLOW BACK ASSEMBLY DIAGRAM

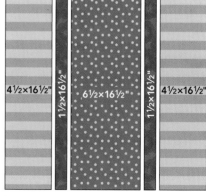

STRIPE PILLOW ASSEMBLY DIAGRAM

From dark red print, cut:
- 2—1½×16½" rectangles

From red dot, cut:
- 2—16½×20½" rectangles
- 1—6½×16½" rectangle

1. Referring to **Stripe Pillow Assembly Diagram**, lay out rectangles. Sew together pieces to make pillow top. Press seams in one direction.

2. Layer pillow top with batting and muslin lining; baste. (For details, see Complete the Quilt, *page 160*.) Quilt as desired. Trim batting and lining even with pillow top edges.

3. Using red dot 16½×20½" rectangles and referring to Cut and Assemble Patchwork Pillow, Step 3, assemble pillow back.

4. Layer pillow top and back with right sides together; join with ¼" seam. Turn right side out. Insert pillow form through opening.

appliqué pillow
materials

- ¼ yard gold dot (block)
- ⅔ yard multicolor floral (block, pillow back)
- ¼ yard green print (border, appliqués)
- ¼ yard dark red print (appliqués)
- 19" square muslin (lining)
- 19" square batting
- 16"-square pillow form
- Lightweight fusible web

Finished pillow: 16" square

Quantities are for 44/45"-wide, 100% cotton fabrics.
Measurements include ¼" seam allowances unless otherwise stated. Sew with right sides together unless otherwise stated.

cut fabrics

Cut pieces in the following order. Patterns can be found on *page 106*. To make templates of the patterns, see Make and Use Templates, *page 158*.

To use fusible web for appliquéing, complete the following steps. (For more information on fusible appliqué, see Piece and Appliqué, *page 158*.)

1. Lay fusible web, paper side up, over patterns. Use a pencil to trace each pattern the number of times indicated in cutting instructions, leaving at least ½" between tracings. Cut out each fusible-web shape roughly ¼" outside traced lines.

2. Following manufacturer's instructions, press fusible-web shapes onto wrong sides of designated fabrics; let cool. Cut out fabric shapes on drawn lines and peel off paper backings.

From gold dot, cut:
- 3—4½×8½" rectangles

From multicolor floral, cut:
- 2—16½×20½" rectangles
- 3—4½" squares

COLOR OPTION

switch 'em
Take a tip from designer Lynette Jensen: Swap the fabrics in a pattern or colorway you love, and you'll create a new look.

From green print, cut:
- 2—2½×16½" border strips
- 2—2½×12½" border strips
- 3 of Pattern B

From dark red print, cut:
- 3 of Pattern A

assemble appliqué pillow

1. Referring to **Appliqué Pillow Assembly Diagram**, lay out gold dot rectangles and multicolor floral squares in three vertical rows. Sew together pieces in each row. Press seams toward multicolor floral squares. Join rows to make a block. Press seams in one direction. The block should be 12½" square including seam allowances.

2. Join green print short border strips to opposite edges of block. Add green print long border strips to remaining edges to make pillow top. Press all seams toward border.

3. Referring to **Appliqué Pillow Assembly Diagram**, position three dark red print A flowers and three green print B flower centers on pillow top. Fuse pieces in place and machine-blanket-stitch with black thread.

4. Layer pillow top with batting and muslin lining; baste. (For details, see Complete the Quilt, *page 160*.) Quilt as desired. Trim batting and lining even with pillow top edges.

5. Using multicolor floral 16½×20½" rectangles and referring to Cut and Assemble Stripe Pillow, steps 3 and 4, *page 104*, assemble pillow back and finish appliqué pillow.

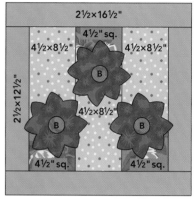

APPLIQUÉ PILLOW ASSEMBLY DIAGRAM

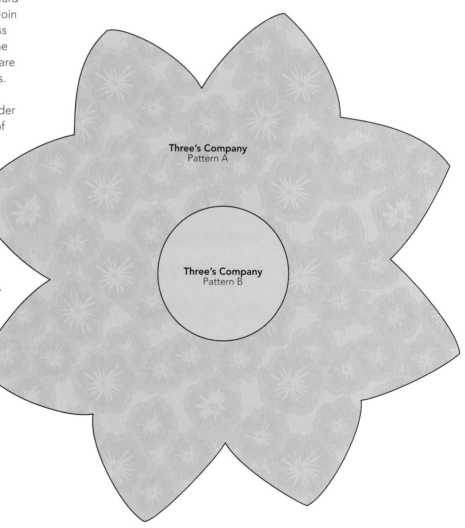

Three's Company
Pattern A

Three's Company
Pattern B

it's a
WRAP

DESIGNER **TARI COLBY**
PHOTOGRAPHER **ADAM ALBRIGHT**

Perk up a pillow and refresh your room decor in
short order with a colorful, easy-to-change band.

materials

- ⅜ yard each of multicolor stripe and circle print (rectangles)
- ⅜ yard complementary print (lining)
- 1½"-diameter wood button
- ¾×9½" piece fusible hook-and-loop tape
- Purchased pillow: 12×20" rectangle

Finished pillow band: 10×28"

Quantities are for 44/45"-wide, 100% cotton fabrics. **Measurements** include ¼" seam allowances. Sew with right sides together unless otherwise stated.

Make seasonal pillow bands to add pizzazz to store-bought pillows. It's as easy as piecing fabric rectangles into a strip, lining them with coordinating fabric, and wrapping them around a pillow for an almost-instant room brightener.

cut fabrics

Cut pieces in the following order.

From multicolor stripe, cut:
- 4—5½×7½" rectangles

From circle print, cut:
- 4—5½×7½" rectangles

From complementary print, cut:
- 1—10½×28½" lining rectangle

assemble pillow wrap

1. Referring to **Diagram 1** for placement, lay out multicolor stripe and circle print rectangles in two rows.

2. Sew together rectangles in each row. Press seams in one direction, alternating direction with remaining row.

3. Join rows to make pillow wrap unit. Press seams in one direction. The pillow wrap unit should be 10½×28½" including seam allowances.

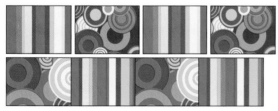

DIAGRAM 1

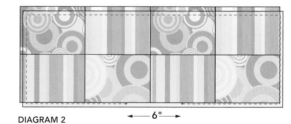

DIAGRAM 2

←— 6" —→

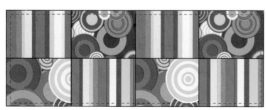

DIAGRAM 3

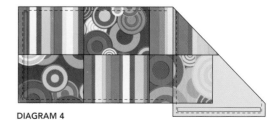

DIAGRAM 4

finish pillow wrap

1. With right sides together, layer pillow wrap unit and 10½×28½" lining rectangle. Stitch around all edges, leaving a 6" opening along one long edge for turning (Diagram 2).

2. Turn right side out through opening and press. Slip-stitch opening closed.

3. Topstitch ⅜" from outer edges to make pillow band (Diagram 3).

4. Pin pillow band around pillow, marking overlap; remove band. Fuse hook-and-loop tape to each short end of pillow band at overlap marks, securing one strip to band's right side and the opposite strip to band's wrong side (Diagram 4).

5. Referring to photo on *page 107*, sew button to pillow band at intersection of center rectangles. Wrap band around pillow and secure using hook-and-loop tape to complete project.

Referring to photo on *page 107*

COLOR OPTION

pillow pizzazz

Pick your favorite fabrics or colorways and whip up a lively band for a plain-Jane pillow in just minutes. The pillow bands shown top to bottom feature feminine fabrics, fun kid-appealing prints, and sophisticated florals.

Whip up this pair of appliqué pillowcases using cheery, contrasting fabrics.

time for BED

DESIGNER **JAN RAGALLER** PHOTOGRAPHER **SCOTT LITTLE**

materials for both pillowcases

- 15" square lightweight fusible web

materials for green pillowcase

- ⅞ yard green-and-pink dot
- ⅓ yard green print
- Scrap of pink print
- Scrap of orange print

materials for blue pillowcase

- ⅞ yard blue-and-yellow dot
- ⅓ yard blue print
- Scrap of yellow print
- Scrap of green print

Finished pillowcase: 30×20" (fits a standard-size pillow)

Quantities are for 44/45"-wide, 100% cotton fabrics.

Measurements include ½" seam allowances. Sew with right sides together unless otherwise stated.

cut fabrics

Cut fabrics in the following order. Letter patterns are on *page 113*. To use fusible web for appliquéing the letters on the pillowcase bands, complete the following steps.

1. Lay fusible web, paper side up, over patterns. Use a pencil to trace each pattern the number of times indicated in cutting instructions, leaving ½" between tracings. Cut out fusible-web shapes roughly ¼" outside traced lines.

2. Following manufacturer's instructions, press each fusible-web shape onto wrong side of designated fabric; let cool. Cut out fabric shapes on drawn lines; peel off paper backings.

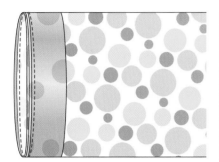

DIAGRAM 1

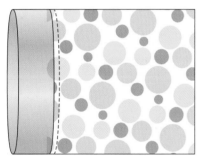

DIAGRAM 2

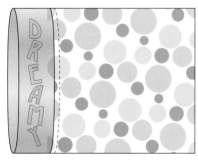

DREAMY PILLOWCASE APPLIQUÉ PLACEMENT DIAGRAM

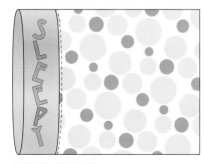

SLEEPY PILLOWCASE APPLIQUÉ PLACEMENT DIAGRAM

For the green pillowcase:
From green-and-pink dot, cut:
- 1—26½×41" rectangle
From green print, cut:
- 1—10×41" strip
From pink print, cut:
- 1 *each* of letters D, R, E, and M
From orange print, cut:
- 1 *each* of letters A and Y

For the blue pillowcase:
From blue-and-yellow dot, cut:
- 1—26½×41" rectangle
From blue print, cut:
- 1—10×41" strip
From yellow print, cut:
- 1 *each* of letters S, E, E, and Y
From green print, cut:
- 1 *each* of letters L and P

assemble pillowcases

1. Using a ½" seam, join short ends of green print 10×41" strip to make a loop. Press seam open.

2. Fold loop in half with wrong sides inside; press to make pillowcase band.

3. Fold green-and-pink dot 26½×41" rectangle in half to form a 26½×20½" rectangle. Sew together long edges and one short end to make pillowcase body. Turn right side out and press flat.

4. Matching raw edges, slide pillowcase band over pillowcase body; pin. Sew together through all layers (Diagram 1).

5. Press pillowcase band open, pressing seams toward pillowcase body. Topstitch ¼" from band edge on pillowcase body to secure the seam allowances and complete pillowcase (Diagram 2).

6. Using the blue-and-yellow polka dot 26½×41" rectangle and the blue print 10×41" strip, repeat steps 1 through 5 for second pillowcase.

finish pillowcases

1. Referring to the **Dreamy Pillowcase Appliqué Placement Diagram** arrange the pink print *D, R, E,* and *M* letters and the orange print *A* and *Y* letters to spell "DREAMY" on the green print pillowcase band. Fuse in place.

2. Using matching thread, machine blanket-stitch with a short stitch length around each appliqué piece.

3. Referring to the **Sleepy Pillowcase Appliqué Placement Diagram** arrange the yellow print letters *S, E,* and *Y* and the green print letters *L* and *P* to spell "SLEEPY" on the blue pillowcase band. Fuse in place.

4. Repeat step 2 to blanket stitch the appliqué pieces on the second pillowcase.

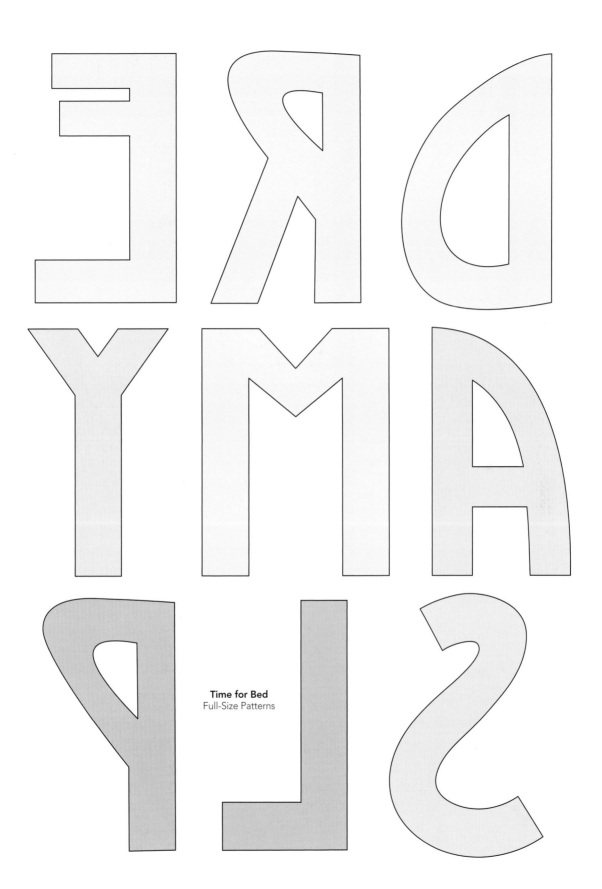

Time for Bed
Full-Size Patterns

pincushions

Fun to make, use, and collect, these easy pincushions can be whipped up in just one evening. They're so pretty, you'll want to keep them on display all the time.

PINCUSHIONS   **115**

It takes just a few fabric bits and buttons to make tiny pin pillows. Give one away, use one to accent your sewing room, or tuck one in your on-the-go sewing kit.

get scrappy

DESIGNER **ROSEANN MEEHAN KERMES**
PHOTOGRAPHER **CAMERON SADEGHPOUR**

materials

- Scraps of light, medium, and dark prints, plaids, and stripes (blocks)
- Polyester fiberfill
- 2—1"-diameter assorted buttons (Square-in-a-Square block)
- 6—½"-diameter assorted buttons (Flying Geese block)

Finished pincushions:
Square-in-a-Square: 3" square
Flying Geese: 3½×7"

Measurements include ¼" seam allowances. Sew with right sides together unless otherwise stated.

Square-in-a-Square or Flying Geese—pick a favorite block and quickly create a sweet, stuffed pin holder with these simple instructions.

cut fabrics for square-in-a-square pincushion

Cut pieces in the following order.

From one light plaid, cut:
- 2—1½" squares, cutting each in half diagonally to make 4 small triangles total

From assorted medium prints, cut:
- 1—3½" square
- 1—2" square

From one dark print, cut:
- 2—2½" squares, cutting each in half diagonally to make 4 large triangles total

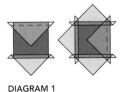

DIAGRAM 1

assemble square-in-a-square pincushion

1. Sew light plaid small triangles to opposite edges of medium print 2" square (**Diagram 1**). Press seams toward triangles. Add light plaid small triangles to remaining edges of square to make block center. Press seams toward triangles. The block center should be 2¾" square including seam allowances.

2. Sew dark print large triangles to opposite edges of block center (**Diagram 2**). Press seams toward large triangles. Add dark print large triangles to remaining edges to make a Square-in-a-Square block; press seams as before. The block should be 3½" square including seam allowances.

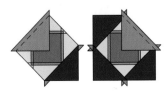

DIAGRAM 2

DIAGRAM 3

DIAGRAM 4

3. Layer Square-in-a-Square block and medium print 3½" square right sides together; stitch around all edges, leaving a 2" opening along one edge for turning. Turn pincushion to right side. Stuff with fiberfill. Slip-stitch opening closed.

4. Center a 1"-diameter button on pincushion top and a second button on the bottom. Taking long stitches through the center of pincushion, sew buttons firmly in place.

cut fabrics for flying geese pincushion

Cut pieces in the following order.

From assorted light, medium, and dark prints, plaids, or stripes, cut:
- 1—4×7½" rectangle
- 4—2¼×4" rectangles
- 8—2¼" squares (4 sets of 2 matching pieces)

assemble flying geese pincushion

1. With a pencil, draw a diagonal line on wrong side of each light, medium, or dark print 2¼" square. (To prevent fabric from stretching as you draw the lines, place 220-grit sandpaper under the squares.)

2. Align a marked 2¼" square with one end of a light, medium, or dark print 2¼×4" rectangle (**Diagram 3**; note placement of marked line). Stitch on marked line; trim excess fabric, leaving ¼" seam allowance. Press open attached triangle.

3. In same manner, sew a matching 2¼" square to opposite end of rectangle (**Diagram 3**; again note placement of marked line). Trim and press as before to make a Flying Geese unit.

4. Repeat steps 2 and 3 to make four Flying Geese units total.

5. Referring to **Diagram 4**, join Flying Geese units in a vertical row to make a Flying Geese block. Press seams in one direction. The block should be 4×7½" including seam allowances.

6. Layer Flying Geese block and light, medium, or dark print 4×7½" rectangle right sides together; join around all edges, leaving a 2" opening along one edge for turning. Turn pincushion to right side. Stuff with fiberfill. Slip-stitch opening closed.

7. Center three ½"-diameter buttons on pincushion top and three on the bottom. Taking long stitches through pincushion, sew buttons firmly in place.

brighten up

Sort through your stash for eye-popping prints to sew up a fun and playful pincushion duo. Make several from seasonal fabrics and they become perfect table favors. Add a hanging loop of perle cotton to make ornaments or package tie-ons for your quilting friends. Cut assorted fabrics for making multiples, then stitch together in assembly-line style. You'll have a basketful of pin pillows ready for last-minute gifts.

editor's tip

To avoid damage to your sewing machine and injury to yourself, don't sew over pins. Remove each pin right before the machine needle gets to it.

DESIGNER **ROSEANN MEEHAN KERMES**
PHOTOGRAPHERS **KRITSADA, MARTY BALDWIN, AND GREG SCHEIDEMANN**

petal
pincushion stacks

These quick-to-make pincushions are cute enough
to give individually or as a towering set of three.

materials

- Scraps of assorted orange-and-green prints
- Embroidery floss: orange or green
- Cotton or polyester fiberfill
- Long, sharp needle (such as a dollmaker's needle)

Finished pincushions:
5½", 4", and 2½" diameter

Quantities are for 100% cotton fabrics.
Measurements include ¼" seam allowances. Sew with right sides together unless otherwise stated.

cut fabrics

Instructions are given to make one large pincushion. For medium or small size, refer to measurements and patterns in parentheses.

Patterns are on *page 123*. To make templates of patterns A and D for large pincushion (B and E for medium; C and F for small), see Make and Use Templates, *page 158*. (Designer Roseann Meehan Kermes quickly cut templates from card stock with an Accu-Cut die-cutting machine, which typically is used to cut shapes for scrapbooking.)

DIAGRAM 1

From assorted orange-and-green prints, cut:

- 2—7" squares (5" squares; 3" squares)
- 1 of Pattern D (E; F)

assemble pincushion

1. On wrong side of an orange-and-green print 7" square (5" square; 3" square), trace around A (B; C) template with a pencil.

2. With right sides together, layer marked and unmarked squares. With a small stitch length (1.5–2 mm), sew on marked line. Overlap stitches slightly where you begin and end.

3. Trim seam allowance a scant ¼" beyond stitching line. Clip corners and curves almost to stitching (**Diagram 1**).

4. Decide which print will be the top of the pincushion; on that side, carefully cut a ¾"-long slit in the center (**Diagram 1**).

black-and-white delights

Black-and-white florals give these pincushions a sleek, modern look. But you needn't stop there. Switch fabric colors and turn the pincushions into spring blooms. Or use holiday prints to make poinsettia pincushions. Create simple ornaments using print fabrics that evoke Victorian designs and the medium and small pincushion templates. Attach a thin gold cord for a hanger.

5. Turn pincushion right side out. Stuff tightly with fiberfill (use eraser end of a pencil to poke stuffing into petals). Hand-stitch opening closed.

finish pincushion

1. Using six strands of orange or green floss and a long, sharp needle, insert needle into pincushion's top center and bring it out at bottom center (**Diagram 2**). Bring floss up around one of the inside curves between petals, then push needle from top center down to bottom center as before. Continue stitching and wrapping floss between all petals, pulling tightly to indent pincushion. Knot securely.

2. Turn under ¼" around orange-and-green print D (E; F) circle.

Using a long running stitch, hand-stitch close to folded edge; draw up stitches tightly and tie thread ends in a knot to make a yo-yo (**Diagram 3**). (To speed process, use large, small, and extra-small yo-yo-making tools available at quilt shops and crafts supply stores.)

3. Hand-stitch yo-yo to top center of pincushion with matching thread to complete pincushion.

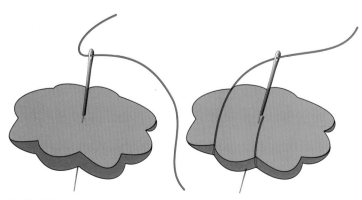

DIAGRAM 2

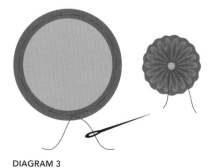

DIAGRAM 3

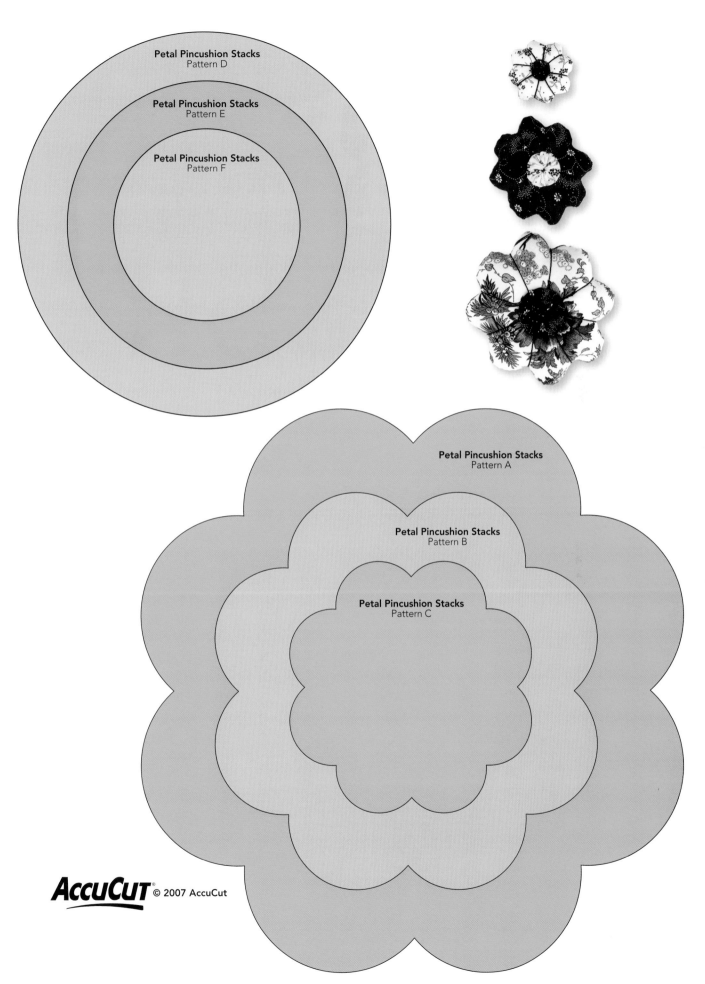

Petal Pincushion Stacks
Pattern D

Petal Pincushion Stacks
Pattern E

Petal Pincushion Stacks
Pattern F

Petal Pincushion Stacks
Pattern A

Petal Pincushion Stacks
Pattern B

Petal Pincushion Stacks
Pattern C

ACCUCUT® © 2007 AccuCut

Almost good enough to eat, these easy cherry-decked pin holders make great gifts for stitching friends.

CHERRIES
on top

DESIGNER **ROSEANN MEEHAN KERMES**
PHOTOGRAPHER **ADAM ALBRIGHT**

---

materials for one each of cherry muffin-top, cherry turnover, and cherry tart pincushions

- 9×16" rectangle pink felted wool (appliqués, background)

- 9×16" rectangle cream felted wool (background)

- Scraps of red, brown, and green felted wool (appliqués)

- Embroidery floss: pink, red, brown, green, and cream

- Polyester fiberfill

- Freezer paper

- Heavy card stock

- ¼"-round paper punch

- Embroidery needle

- 3½"-diameter ceramic ramekin or soufflé dish (optional)

Cherry muffin-top pincushion:
3½" diameter
Cherry turnover pincushion: 3½×7"
Cherry tart pincushion:
4½" diameter

Quantities are for 100% wool fabrics.

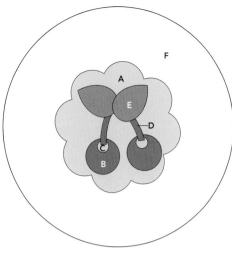

CHERRY MUFFIN-TOP
APPLIQUÉ PLACEMENT DIAGRAM

COUCHING STITCH
DIAGRAM

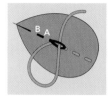

RUNNING STITCH
DIAGRAM

Indulge in all the sweets you like. These pastries, so beautiful they make your mouth water, are actually delightful pincushions made of felted wool.

prepare fabrics

Felted wool doesn't fray, so there is no need to turn under the edges of appliqué pieces. To felt wool, machine-wash it in a hot-water-wash, cool-rinse cycle with a small amount of detergent; machine-dry on high heat and steam-press.

cut fabrics for cherry muffin-top pincushion

Cut pieces in the following order. Patterns are on *pages 129–130.*

To use freezer paper for cutting appliqué shapes, complete the following steps.

1. Lay freezer paper, shiny side down, over patterns. Use a pencil to trace each pattern the number of times indicated in cutting instructions, leaving ½" between tracings. Cut out freezer-paper shapes roughly ¼" outside traced lines.

2. Using a hot dry iron, press freezer-paper shapes, shiny sides down, onto right sides of designated wools; let cool. Cut out wool shapes on drawn lines. Use a ¼"-round paper punch to cut small interior holes in scallop trim (Pattern H). Peel off freezer paper.

From pink wool, cut:
- 1 each of patterns A and H
- 2 of Pattern C

From cream wool, cut:
- 1 each of patterns F and G

From red wool, cut:
- 2 of Pattern B

From brown wool, cut:
- 2 of Pattern D

From green wool, cut:
- 2 of Pattern E

From heavy card stock, cut:
- 1 of Pattern G

appliqué and assemble cherry muffin-top pincushion

1. Referring to **Cherry Muffin-Top Appliqué Placement Diagram,** center pink wool A scalloped circle on cream wool F circle; pin in place. Using one strand of pink embroidery floss, whipstitch pink circle in place.

2. Referring to **Cherry Muffin-Top Appliqué Placement Diagram,** position two red wool B cherries, two pink wool C circles, two brown wool D stems, and two green wool E leaves on scalloped circle; pin in place.

3. Use one strand of red embroidery floss to whipstitch around cherries. Use one strand of pink embroidery floss to whipstitch around C circles.

4. Use one strand of brown embroidery floss to couch stems in place.

   To make a couching stitch, work small stitches about ⅛" apart back and forth over the stem (**Couching Stitch Diagram**).

5. Use one strand of green embroidery floss and a running stitch to sew down center of leaves to complete pincushion top.

   To make a running stitch, pull needle up at A and insert it back into fabric at B (**Running Stitch Diagram**).

6. Thread an embroidery needle with 36" of sewing thread; knot ends together. Work ⅛"-long

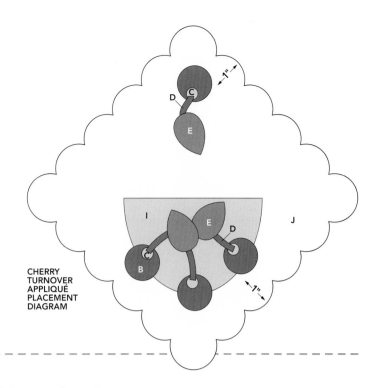

CHERRY TURNOVER APPLIQUÉ PLACEMENT DIAGRAM

editor's tip

If you are working with wool for the first time, be aware that when you felt wool, one yard of 54"-wide wool will shrink to a soft and fluffy piece approximately 32×52".

gathering stitches about ¼" from edge of pincushion top. Pull up threads to gather slightly.

7. Place fiberfill in center of wrong side of pincushion top; position card stock G circle atop fiberfill and pull gathers tight around card stock circle. Secure thread. (Turn pincushion top over to check firmness. If necessary, relax gathers and add more fiberfill before securing thread.)

8. Place a small amount of fiberfill in center of card stock circle, then position cream wool G circle over fiberfill (circle should cover gathering stitches on pincushion).

9. Use one strand of cream embroidery floss to whipstitch pincushion top and cream wool G circle together along edges.

10. Pin pink wool H scallop strip around pincushion, overlapping ends slightly. Whipstitch top edge of scallop strip to finish pincushion. If desired, place in a 3½"-diameter ceramic ramekin or soufflé dish.

cut fabrics for cherry turnover pincushion

Cut pieces in the following order. Patterns are on *pages 129–130*.

For details on felting wool, see Prepare Fabrics, *page 126*. To use freezer paper for cutting appliqué shapes, see Cut Fabrics for Cherry Muffin-Top Pincushion, *page 126*.

From cream wool, cut:
- 1 of Pattern J

From pink wool, cut:
- 1 of Pattern I
- 4 of Pattern C

From red wool, cut:
- 4 of Pattern B

From brown wool, cut:
- 4 of Pattern D

From green wool, cut:
- 3 of Pattern E

appliqué and assemble cherry turnover pincushion

1. Fold cream wool J piece in half diagonally; lightly press. Open flat.

2. Referring to **Cherry Turnover Appliqué Placement Diagram**, center pink wool I semicircle on J piece with straight edge of

semicircle along pressed fold; pin in place. Use one strand of pink embroidery floss to whipstitch semicircle in place.

3. Referring to **Cherry Turnover Appliqué Placement Diagram**, position four red wool B cherries, four pink wool C circles, four brown wool D stems, and three green wool E leaves on J piece; pin in place.

4. Use one strand of red embroidery floss to whipstitch around cherries. Use one strand of pink embroidery floss to whipstitch around C circles.

5. Referring to Appliqué and Assemble Cherry Muffin-Top Pincushion, Step 4, couch stems in place.

6. Referring to Appliqué and Assemble Cherry Muffin-Top Pincushion, Step 5, sew leaves in place with a running stitch.

7. With wrong sides together, refold J piece in half diagonally to make a triangle.

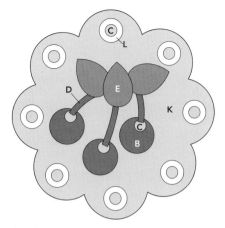

CHERRY TART
APPLIQUÉ PLACEMENT DIAGRAM

BLANKET STITCH DIAGRAM

FRENCH KNOT DIAGRAM

8. Using two strands of pink embroidery floss and a running stitch, begin at one corner of triangle and sew through both layers ¾" in from scalloped edge, leaving a 1½" opening for stuffing. Do not clip thread.

9. Stuff pincushion firmly with fiberfill. Continue stitching both layers together, then secure thread, hiding knot inside.

   To blanket-stitch, pull needle up at A, form a reverse L shape with floss, and hold angle of L shape in place with your thumb (**Blanket Stitch Diagram**). Push needle down at B and come up at C to secure stitch. Continue in same manner.

cut fabrics for cherry tart pincushion

Cut pieces in the following order. Patterns are on *pages 129–130*.

   For details on felting wool, see Prepare Fabrics, *page 126*. To use freezer paper for cutting appliqué shapes, see Cut Fabrics for Cherry Muffin-Top Pincushion, *page 126*.

From cream wool, cut:
- 8 of Pattern L

From red wool, cut:
- 3 of Pattern B

From pink wool, cut:
- 2 of Pattern K
- 11 of Pattern C

From brown wool, cut:
- 3 of Pattern D

From green wool, cut:
- 3 of Pattern E

appliqué and assemble cherry tart pincushion

1. Referring to **Cherry Tart Appliqué Placement Diagram**, position three red wool B cherries, three pink wool C circles, three brown wool D stems, and three green wool E leaves in center of a pink wool K scalloped circle; pin in place.

2. Use one strand of red embroidery floss to whipstitch around cherries. Use one strand of pink embroidery floss to whipstitch around C circles.

3. Referring to Appliqué and Assemble Cherry Muffin-Top Pincushion, Step 4, couch stems in place.

4. Referring to Appliqué and Assemble Cherry Muffin-Top Pincushion, Step 5, sew leaves in place with a running stitch.

5. Referring to **Cherry Tart Appliqué Placement Diagram**, stack a cream wool L circle and a pink wool C circle in each scallop of pink wool K piece.

6. Using two strands of red embroidery floss, stitch a French knot in center of each circle stack to secure.

   To make a French knot, pull needle and floss through at point where knot is desired (A on **French Knot Diagram**). Wrap floss around needle twice without twisting it. Insert tip of needle into fabric at B, about ¹⁄₁₆" away from A. Gently push wraps down needle to meet fabric. Pull needle and trailing floss through fabric slowly and smoothly.

7. Using two strands of pink embroidery floss, blanket-stitch edges of appliquéd K piece and remaining K piece together, leaving a ½" opening for stuffing. Do not clip thread.

8. Stuff firmly with fiberfill. Continue stitching both layers together, then secure thread, hiding knot inside to finish pincushion.

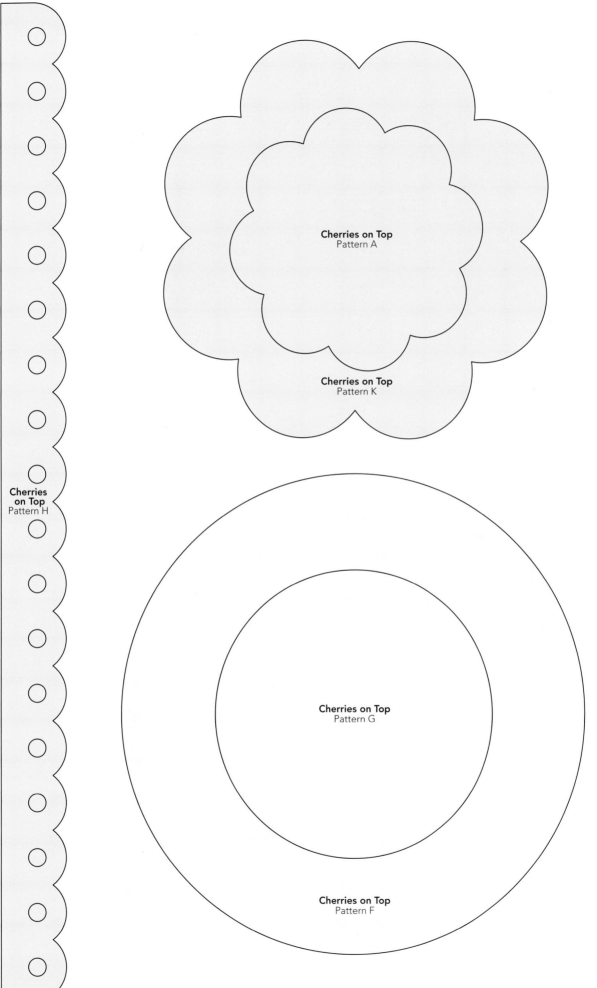

Cherries on Top
Pattern A

Cherries on Top
Pattern K

Cherries on Top
Pattern H

Cherries on Top
Pattern G

Cherries on Top
Pattern F

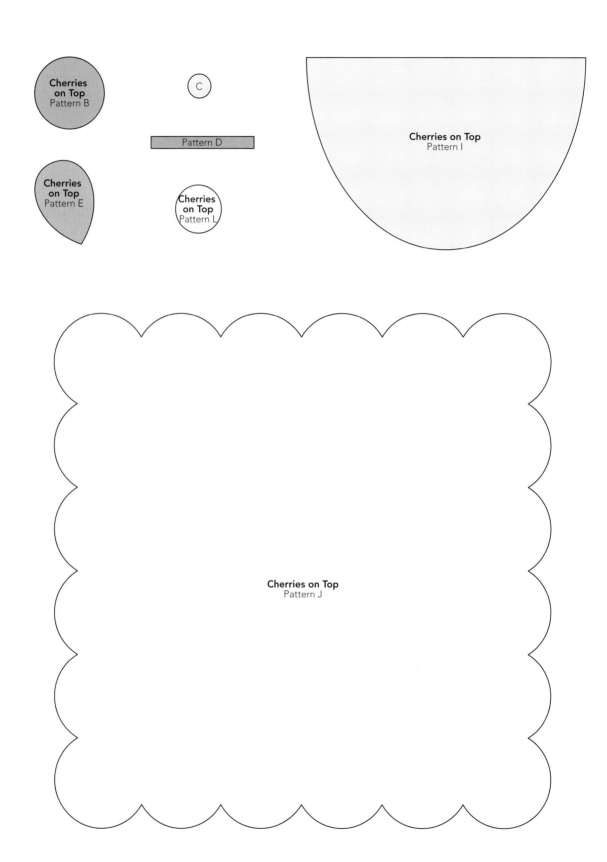

Cherries
on Top
Pattern B

C

Pattern D

Cherries
on Top
Pattern E

Cherries
on Top
Pattern L

Cherries on Top
Pattern I

Cherries on Top
Pattern J

DESIGNER **ANNA MARIA HORNER**
PHOTOGRAPHERS **GREG SCHEIDEMANN AND JASON DONNELLY**

wild flowers

Snip, stitch, and stuff. Soon you will have
a garden of flower pincushions.

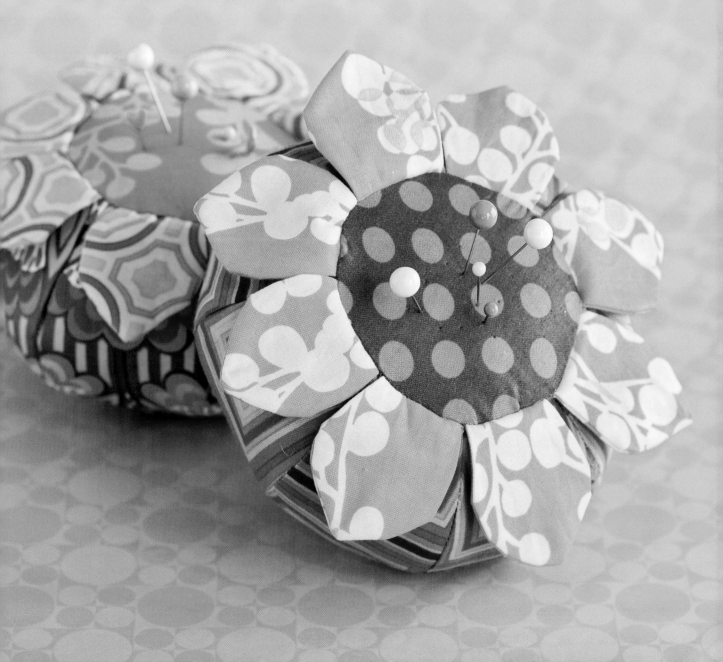

materials

- ¼ yard multicolor print (pincushion sides, bottom)
- ⅛ yard orange floral (petals)
- 6" square magenta polka dot (center)
- 6" square heavy interfacing
- Polyester fiberfill

Finished pincushion: 6×6×3"

Quantities are for 44/45"-wide, 100% cotton fabrics.
Measurements include ¼" seam allowances. Sew with right sides together unless otherwise stated.

These pincushions are so much fun to sew. Choose a mix of your favorite fabrics, pile on the petals, and watch your garden grow—dozens of fanciful pincushions could sprout up over a weekend.

cut fabrics

Cut pieces in the following order. The patterns are on *Pattern Sheet 2*. To make templates of the patterns, see Make and Use Templates on *page 158*.

From multicolor print, cut:
- 8 of Pattern A
- 1 of Pattern D

From orange floral, cut:
- 16 of Pattern B

From magenta polka dot, cut:
- 1 of Pattern C

From heavy interfacing, cut:
- 1 of Pattern C

assemble pincushion

1. Sew together multicolor print A pieces in a row to make pincushion side (**Diagram 1**). Clip seam allowances; finger-press seams to one side.

2. Join two orange floral B pieces, leaving short edge open for turning (**Diagram 2**). Turn right side out. Press to make a petal. Repeat to make eight petals total.

3. Matching center marks at raw edges, pin petals to outside of pincushion side; baste (**Diagram 3**).

4. Sew together ends of pincushion side to make a circle, leaving an opening for stuffing (**Diagram 4**).

5. Matching dots, baste magenta polka-dot C circle to top edge of pincushion side (**Diagram 5**). Join together ¼" from edge. Clip seams; turn to right side.

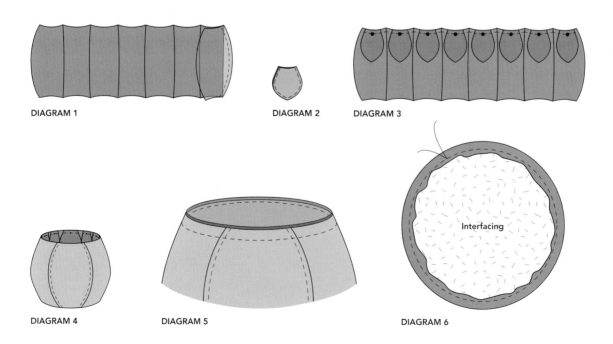

DIAGRAM 1

DIAGRAM 2

DIAGRAM 3

DIAGRAM 4

DIAGRAM 5

Interfacing

DIAGRAM 6

6. Stuff lightly with fiberfill until pincushion stands on its own.

7. Baste small gathering stitches ⅛" from edges of multicolor print D circle. Center interfacing C circle on wrong side of D circle; pull gathers tight, wrapping D circle around interfacing, to make pincushion base (**Diagram 6**). Secure thread. Press.

8. Hand-sew pincushion base to bottom opening.

9. Stuff firmly with fiberfill. Hand-sew side opening closed to complete pincushion.

too many pincushions?

Impossible! But if your sewing room is fast filling up with your pincushion collection, fill these pretty posies with lavender for a sweet sachet. Or, fill one with flaxseed. Then warm up or chill the finished cushion for a stress reducer that's just the right size for a stiff shoulder or knee.

editor's tip

Use a short stitch length (1.5 to 2 mm) when sewing the sides and top of these rounded pincushions. Tiny stitches will help reinforce the seams and prevent the stitches from popping when you add the stuffing.

flight
of fancy

Given as a gift or whipped up for yourself, this felted wool pincushion features simple embroidery stitches and loads of charm.

DESIGNER **KIMBER MITCHELL VAN HEUKELOM**
PHOTOGRAPHER **SCOTT LITTLE**

materials

- 2—8" squares of pink houndstooth wool (body)
- Scraps of off-white, light pink, brown, light blue, light green, and dark pink wool (leaves, flowers, bird, and bird wing)
- 1×20" light blue wool strip, cutting one long edge with scalloped decorative-edge scissors (pincushion edge)
- Embroidery floss: brown, pink, light blue, yellow, white
- Size 8 perle cotton: pink and brown
- 1—½"-diameter button: white (flower center)
- 1—⅝"-diameter button: brown (flower center)
- 3—⅜"-diameter buttons: light blue, pink, and yellow (flower centers)
- 1 micro button: off-white (bird eye)
- Pinking shears and scalloped decorative-edge shears
- Needles: embroidery and beading
- White sewing thread
- Polyester fiberfill
- Freezer paper
- Fabric glue

Finished Pincushion: 6¼" diameter

Measurements include ¼" seam allowances. Sew with right sides together.

prepare fabrics

Felted wool (available in many quilt shops) doesn't fray, so there is no need to turn under the edges of appliqué pieces. If you want to felt your own wool, machine-wash it in a hot-water-wash, cool-rinse cycle with a small amount of detergent; machine-dry it on high heat and steam-press.

cut fabrics

Cut the pieces in the following order. Patterns are on *Pattern Sheet 2*.

To use freezer paper for cutting appliqué shapes, complete the following steps.

1. Lay freezer paper, shiny side down, over patterns. Use a pencil to trace each pattern the number of times indicated in cutting instructions, leaving ½" between tracings. Cut out each freezer-paper shape roughly ¼" outside traced lines.

2. Using a hot, dry iron, press each freezer-paper shape, shiny side down, onto right side of the designated wools; let cool.

3. Cut out the brown wool G piece on the drawn lines. For remaining G wool pieces, align the deepest point of either the pinking or scalloped decorative-edge shears with the drawn line. Use the pinking shears to cut out the light green and the off-white wool G pieces. Use scalloped decorative-edge shears to cut out the light blue and dark pink wool G pieces.

4. Cut out the light blue wool F and off-white wool B pieces with pinking shears, using the drawn line as a guide.

5. Cut out all other wool shapes on the drawn lines. Peel off freezer paper.

From pink houndstooth wool, cut:
- 2 of Pattern A

From off-white wool scrap, cut:
- 1 of Pattern B
- 1 of Pattern G

From light pink wool scrap, cut:
- 1 of Pattern C

From brown wool scrap, cut:
- 1 of Pattern D
- 1 of Pattern G

From light blue wool scrap, cut:
- 1 of Pattern E
- 1 of Pattern F
- 1 of Pattern G

From light green wool scrap, cut:
- 1 of Pattern G
- 1 of Pattern H

From dark pink wool scrap, cut:
- 1 of Pattern G

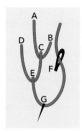

FEATHER STITCH

FRENCH KNOT

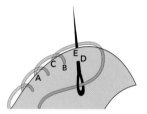

BLANKET STITCH

RUNNING STITCH

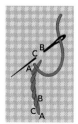

STEM STITCH

appliqué pincushion top

1. Referring to the **Appliqué Placement Diagram** *opposite*, baste the pinked off-white B piece to the pink houndstooth wool A piece. Baste it so the stitches will be hidden beneath the light pink wool C piece once it is attached.

2. Using fabric glue, adhere the light pink wool C piece on top of the pinked off-white wool B piece.

3. Using two strands of brown embroidery floss, add a feather stitch through the center of the light pink wool C piece.

   To complete a feather stitch, pull needle up at A, form a V shape with floss, and hold the angle in place with your thumb **(Feather Stitch Diagram).** Push needle down at B, about 3/8" from A, and come up at C. For the next stitch, insert needle at D and bring it up at E; continue in the same manner.

4. Using fabric glue, attach the brown wool D piece to the light blue wool E piece. Allow to dry.

5. Referring to the photo on *page 134,* use two strands of pink embroidery floss to make three French knots on the brown wool D piece.

   To make a French knot, pull thread through at point where knot is desired (A) **(French Knot Diagram).** Wrap thread around needle six times without twisting it. Insert tip of needle into fabric at B, 1/16" away from A. Gently push wraps down needle to meet fabric. Pull needle and trailing thread through fabric slowly and smoothly.

6. Using a blanket stitch and two strands of pink embroidery floss, sew the light blue E piece to the pink houndstooth wool A piece. When you get to the wing, simply take a deeper stitch to catch the bottom part of the wing in two spots (see photo on *page 134*).

   To blanket stitch, pull your needle up at A, form a reverse L shape with floss, and hold angle of L shape in place with your thumb **(Blanket Stitch Diagram).** Push your needle down at B and come up at C to secure stitch. Continue in the same manner.

7. For the bird eye, use white sewing thread and a beading needle to attach a micro button to the light blue wool E piece.

8. Referring to the **Appliqué Placement Diagram,** place the pinked blue wool F piece on the pincushion top. Then position a scalloped pink wool G piece on top of the F piece. Place a white button on top of the G piece and sew through the layers with white sewing thread.

9. Referring to the **Appliqué Placement Diagram,** overlap the brown wool G piece with the light green wool H piece. Using a blanket stitch and two strands of yellow embroidery floss, stitch the brown wool G piece to the pincushion top.

   To blanket stitch, see step 6.
   Using a feather stitch and two strands of brown embroidery floss, stitch through the center of the light green wool H piece.
   To feather stitch, see step 3.
   Attach a yellow button to the center of the flower with yellow floss.

10. Referring to the **Appliqué Placement Diagram**, place a pinked off-white wool G piece on the pincushion top.

    Using a running stitch and one strand of light blue embroidery floss, sew about ⅛" from the edge of the scalloped off-white wool G piece through all layers. Attach a light blue button to the center of the flower with light blue floss.

    To complete a running stitch, pull needle up at A and insert it back into fabric at B (**Running Stitch Diagram**, *opposite*). Continue in the same manner, loading several stitches on the needle at a time.

11. Referring to the **Appliqué Placement Diagram**, place a scalloped light blue wool G piece on the pincushion body. Sew a pink button through the center of the G piece to the pincushion body using pink floss.

12. Referring to the **Appliqué Placement Diagram**, repeat Step 11 using a pinked light green wool G piece, a brown button, and brown floss.

13. Referring to the **Appliqué Placement Diagram**, use a stem stitch and brown perle cotton to connect the flowers.

    To stem-stitch, pull your needle up at A, then insert it back into fabric at B, about ⅜" away from A (**Stem Stitch Diagram**, *opposite*). Holding floss out of the way, bring your needle back up at C and pull floss through so it lies flat against fabric.

The distances between points A, B, and C should be equal. Pull gently with equal tautness after each stitch. Continue in the same manner, holding floss out of the way on same side of stitching every time.

assemble pincushion

1. With right sides together, sew the appliquéd pincushion top with the remaining pink houndstooth wool A piece, leaving a 2" opening for turning. Backstitch at beginning and end of seam. Clip curves. Turn right side out.

2. Stuff the pincushion firmly with fiberfill.

3. Using two strands of embroidery floss, whipstitch the opening closed.

4. Apply fabric glue to the wrong side of the light blue wool 1×20" strip. With scalloped-edge down, attach the strip along the seam line of the pincushion, concealing the seam and leaving the last one inch of the strip unattached. Trim the end of the strip to fit snugly against the beginning of the strip; glue the strip end in place.

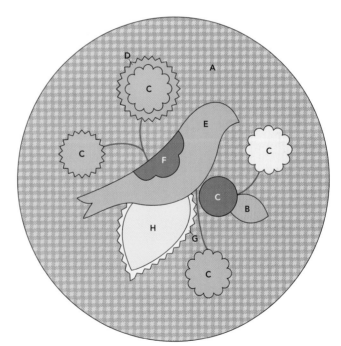

APPLIQUÉ PLACEMENT DIAGRAM

big&BOLD

Don't spend time searching for your pincushion. Make a jumbo, tufted cushion in bright, lively prints and finding it will be a cinch!

DESIGNER **JILL ABELOE MEAD**
PHOTOGRAPHERS **CAMERON SADEGHPOUR**
AND MARTY BALDWIN

materials
- 18×22" piece (fat quarter) red print (pincushion top and bottom)
- 18×22" piece (fat quarter) red polka dot (pincushion side, button)
- 2—18×22" pieces fusible interfacing
- Polyester fiberfill
- 2—1½"-diameter buttons to cover
- Dollmaker's needle
- Water-soluble marking pen

Finished pincushion: 6×6×3"

Quantities are for 44/45"-wide, 100% cotton fabrics. **Measurements** include ¼" seam allowances. Sew with right sides together unless otherwise stated.

To make the sides of the pincushion extra-durable, apply fusible interfacing to each fabric piece before cutting out the pattern pieces.

cut fabrics
Cut pieces in the following order. Patterns are on *Pattern Sheet 2.* (Pattern B has two sections. To make a full-size pattern measuring 12½" long, trace both sections on one large sheet of paper, overlapping shaded areas.)

To make templates of the patterns, see Make and Use Templates, *page 158.* Be sure to transfer the dots (matching points) marked on the patterns to the templates, then to the fabric pieces.

Following manufacturer's instructions, fuse each red print and red polka dot 18×22" rectangle to a fusible interfacing 18×22" rectangle to reinforce pattern pieces; let cool.

From fused red print, cut:
- 2 of Pattern A

From fused red polka dot, cut:
- 2 *each* of Patterns B and C

assemble pincushion

1. Using sharp scissors, clip into seam allowance along edges of red polka dot B strips at marked dots, but do not cut into or beyond seam lines.

2. Layer and sew together B pieces across each short end to make a loop. Press seams open.

3. Matching dots, sew one long edge of loop to a red print A square.

4. Repeat Step 3, joining remaining red print A square to unsewn edge of loop, leaving a 2" opening along one edge for turning.

5. Turn pincushion right side out. Stuff firmly with fiberfill. Hand-sew opening closed.

6. Following manufacturer's instructions, cover each button using a red polka dot C circle.

7. Thread dollmaker's needle with double length of thread; knot end. Stitch down through center of pincushion; sew through button shank of first button and back through center of pincushion. Sew through button shank of second button on opposite side of pincushion. Repeat as needed, pulling thread tight to gather pincushion at center. Tie off ends of thread.

wool &
whimsy

Love to work with wool?
Bring garden-fresh blooms to
any sewing table with folk
art wool pincushions that you
can stitch in an afternoon.

DESIGNER **ROSEANN MEEHAN KERMES**
PHOTOGRAPHER **CAMERON SADEGHPOUR**

large pincushion

materials

- 5×9" rectangle pink felted wool (background)

- Scraps of green, yellow, dark pink, turquoise, red, blue, and orange felted wools (appliqués)

- 2—6½×9½" rectangles teal plaid felted wool (pincushion)

- Embroidery floss: green, dark pink, and gold

- Polyester fiberfill

- Freezer paper

Finished pincushion: 6×9"

Quantities are for 100% wool fabrics.

cut fabrics

Felted wool (available in many quilt shops) doesn't fray, so there is no need to turn under the edges of the appliqué shapes. To felt your own wool, machine-wash it in a hot-water-wash, cool-rinse cycle with a small amount of detergent; machine-dry it on high heat and steam-press.

To make the best use of your fabrics, cut the pieces in the following order.

Patterns are on *pages 144–145*. To use freezer paper for cutting appliqué shapes, complete the following steps. (To use fusible web when cutting shapes, see "Using Fusible Web with Wool," *page 145*.)

1. Lay freezer paper, shiny side down, over patterns. Use a pencil to trace each pattern the number of times indicated, leaving ½" between tracings. Cut out freezer-paper shapes roughly ¼" outside the traced lines.

2. Using a hot, dry iron, press freezer-paper shapes, shiny side down, onto designated fabrics; let cool. Cut out fabric shapes on drawn lines and peel off freezer paper.

From pink wool, cut:
- 1 of Pattern E

From green wool, cut:
- 1—¼×5" strip for stem
- 1 of Pattern D

From yellow, dark pink, turquoise, red, blue, and orange wool scraps, cut:
- 1 *each* of patterns A, B, and C
- 5 of Pattern D

editor's tip

Couching is an easy, yet attractive, way to attach narrow wool pieces, thick threads, ribbons, and other trims to a surface.

---

appliqué and assemble large pincushion

1. Referring to **Appliqué Placement Diagram,** position green wool ¼×5" stem on pink wool E background; baste in place.

2. Using two strands of green embroidery floss and a couching stitch, sew stem in place.

   To make a couching stitch, work small stitches, ¼" to ⅜" apart, back and forth over the strip (**Couching Diagram**).

3. Position A flower on background; pin. Using one strand of dark pink floss and a running stitch, sew A flower in place.

To make a running stitch, pull needle up at A and insert it back into fabric at B (**Running Stitch Diagram**). Continue in same manner, loading several stitches on needle at a time.

4. Referring to **Appliqué Placement Diagram,** position B and C pieces on center of A flower. Using two strands of gold floss and a star stitch, sew both pieces in place.

   To make a star stitch, pull needle up at A and push it down at B (**Star Stitch Diagram**). Bring needle up at C, cross it over first stitch, and push needle down at D. Pull needle up at E and push it down at F.

5. Using two strands of gold floss, add a French knot at center of C piece.

To make a French knot, pull the floss through at A, the point where the knot is desired (**French Knot Diagram**). Wrap the thread around needle two or three times without twisting it. Insert the tip of needle into fabric at B, ¹⁄₁₆" away from A. Gently push the wraps down the needle to meet fabric. Pull needle and trailing floss through the fabric slowly and smoothly. The size of a French knot depends on the number of floss strands and how many times you wrap them around the needle.

6. Referring to **Appliqué Placement Diagram,** position D leaves along stem; pin. Using one strand of green or gold floss and a backstitch, sew each leaf in place.

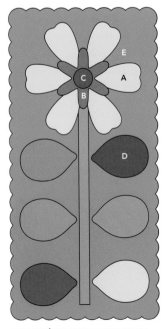

APPLIQUÉ PLACEMENT DIAGRAM

COUCHING

RUNNING STITCH

STAR STITCH

FRENCH KNOT

BACKSTITCH

To backstitch, pull needle up at A (**Backstitch Diagram**, *opposite*). Insert it back into fabric at B and bring it up at C. Push needle down again at D and bring it up at E. Continue in same manner.

7. Referring to photo on *page 141*, pin appliquéd background to a teal plaid 6½×9½" rectangle. Using one strand of dark pink floss, tack-stitch along scalloped edges to make pincushion top.

    To tack-stitch, pull needle up at A and push it down at B (**Tack Stitch Diagram**). Come up at C and continue in same manner around entire appliqué shape.

8. With right sides together, sew together pincushion top and remaining teal plaid 6½×9½" rectangle, leaving a small opening for turning. Trim corners.

9. Turn right side out. Using a chopstick or the eraser end of a pencil, push out corners. Stuff pincushion firmly with fiberfill. Whipstitch opening closed to complete large pincushion.

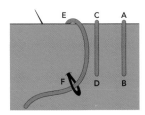

TACK STITCH

small pincushion

materials

- Scraps of dark purple, turquoise, and yellow felted wools (appliqués)
- 6" square pink felted wool (pincushion)
- Embroidery floss: pink
- Polyester fiberfill
- Freezer paper
- Heavy card stock
- Sewing thread
- Embroidery needle

Finished pincushion: 3¼"-diameter

Quantities are for 100% wool fabrics.

cut fabrics

To make the best use of your fabrics, cut the pieces in the following order. Patterns are on *pages 144–145*. To use freezer paper for cutting appliqué shapes and for details on felting your own wool, see Cut Fabrics, *page 140*.

From dark purple, turquoise, and yellow felted wool scraps, cut:
- 1 *each* of patterns A, B, and C

From pink felted wool, cut:
- 1 *each* of patterns F and G

From heavy card stock, cut:
- 1 of Pattern F

editor's tip

When you're finished constructing the small pincushion, house it inside a muffin tin along with other sewing notions for a fun and handy addition to your sewing space.

- -

appliqué and assemble small pincushion

1. Referring to Appliqué and Assemble Large Pincushion, steps 3 and 4, *page 142*, and using one strand of pink embroidery floss, appliqué flower pieces to pink G background to make pincushion top.

2. Cut sewing thread about 24" to 36" long. Thread length through an embroidery needle and knot ends. Work small, even gathering stitches, about ⅛" long, around pincushion top about ¼" from edge.

3. With right side down, place a small amount of fiberfill in center of pincushion top; position card stock F piece on top and pull gathers tight around card stock circle. Secure thread. *Note:* Turn pincushion top over to check firmness. You may need to relax gathers and add more fiberfill before securing thread.

4. Place a small amount of fiberfill in center of card stock circle.

5. Position pink F piece over fiberfill. *Note:* Pink F piece should cover gathering stitches.

6. Using one strand of pink floss, tack-stitch pincushion top and pink F piece together along edges to complete small pincushion.

    To tack-stitch, see Appliqué and Assemble Large Pincushion, Step 7, *page 143*.

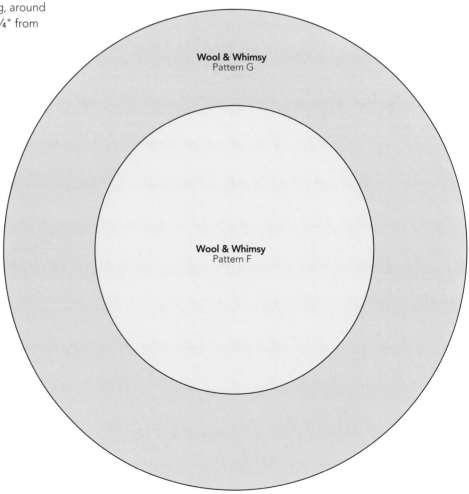

Wool & Whimsy
Pattern G

Wool & Whimsy
Pattern F

using fusible web with wool

A lightweight, paper-backed fusible web, when fused to wool, also can provide stability when cutting out small or intricate shapes.

To use fusible web, complete the following steps.

Lay fusible web, paper side up, over patterns. Use a pencil to trace each pattern the number of times indicated in cutting instructions, leaving ½" between tracings. Cut out each fusible-web shape roughly ¼" outside traced lines.

Following manufacturer's instructions, press fusible-web shapes onto designated wools; let cool.

Cut out wool shapes on drawn lines and peel off paper backings.

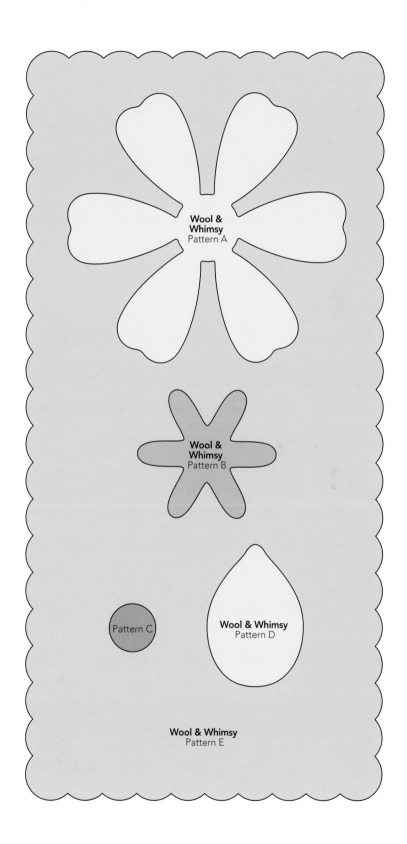

Wool &
Whimsy
Pattern A

Wool &
Whimsy
Pattern B

Pattern C

Wool & Whimsy
Pattern D

Wool & Whimsy
Pattern E

flower
wristband

Layers of rolled-up wool roving form
the pincushion center of this pretty
floral wristband.

DESIGNER **VICKIE CLONTZ**
PHOTOGRAPHER **MARTY BALDWIN**

materials for one pincushion

- 100% wool roving 2×18" lengths in lavender, pink, strawberry
- 1½×12" strip of green cotton fabric
- 2×12" strip of rose-colored Woolfelt or felted wool
- ¼ yard of ¼"-wide elastic
- Old knee-high stocking
- Safety pin or bodkin

Finished pincushion: 4" round

cut fabrics

The pattern is on *Pattern Sheet 1*. From rose-colored Woolfelt or felted wool, cut:

- 6 of Petal Pattern

make the pincushion

1. Lay out the wool roving in layers, with the lavender fibers on the bottom, pink fibers in the middle, and strawberry fibers on top. Align the layers so the edges are fairly even and the lavender fibers are an inch or two longer on one end.

2. Beginning at the opposite end, roll the roving tightly like a jelly-roll, keeping the sides even. When you reach the end, smooth the lavender fibers out so the entire side of the wool roll is lavender with the swirls on the top and bottom. Holding the roll in one hand, carefully stuff it into the toe of a knee-high stocking. Tie a knot snugly above the roll.

3. Wash the stocking in a washing machine in warm or hot soapy water. Rinse in cold water, then dry in a clothes dryer. Repeat two more times for a total of three wash/dry cycles.

4. When the roll is completely dry, cut the knot off the stocking. Carefully pull the stocking off the entangled fibers of the roll. Trim off the fuzz using sharp scissors.

5. Hold the roll sideways on a cutting surface with the inside swirl perpendicular to the cutting surface. Using a very sharp knife, cut ½" off of one swirly end of the roll using a gentle, continuous sawing motion. To avoid a jagged edge, do not remove the blade from the roll until you have cut completely through it. Clean up uneven cut edges with scissors. The roll pincushion should be about 1" deep.

6. Lay out six rose-colored petal pieces in a row so all straight edges are alligned and petals are slightly overlapped. Using a long stitch, hand-sew about ⅛" from straight ends, leaving thread ends long.

PETAL ASSEMBLY DIAGRAM

Pull up thread to gather (**Petal Assembly Diagram**). Pin the petals to the underside of the pincushion, leaving a ½" open circle in the center. Sew the petals to the pincushion by hand.

make the wristband

1. Press all edges of the green 2×12" strip under ¼" to the wrong side. Press strip in half lengthwise.

2. With wrong sides together, sew the long folded edges together to make a casing for the elastic. Use a safety pin or bodkin to attach to one end of the elastic and pull it through the casing. Fit the casing around your wrist with elastic ends overlapping ½"; trim elastic. Sew the overlapped elastic ends together. Whipstitch the casing ends together.

3. Sew the wristband to underside of pincushion between the petals.

Make your own fancy pins by gluing glass beads onto the end of a doll-making needle. Use glass and bead adhesive to hold them securely in place.

Appliqué and stuff a felted wool circle to serve up a zero-calorie pin catcher. This to-go treat is easily assembled and embellished on the fly with basic hand stitches.

pincushion *parfait*

DESIGNER **VICKIE CLONTZ**
PHOTOGRAPHER **GREG SCHEIDEMANN**

materials for one pincushion

- 4" square brown felted wool (appliqué)
- 9" square pink felted wool (pincushion)
- 3" square white felted wool (appliqué)
- Embroidery floss: brown
- ½"-diameter button: red
- Polyester fiberfill
- Freezer paper
- Embroidery needle
- 4"-diameter, 5"-tall parfait glass (optional)
- ¼ cup each white and pink assorted buttons (optional)

Finished pincushion:
3½" diameter, 2" high

Quantities are for 100% wool or 50/50 felted wool-blend fabrics.

prepare fabrics

Felted wool doesn't fray, so there is no need to turn under the edges of the appliqué pieces.

To felt wool, machine-wash it in a hot-water-wash, cool-rinse cycle with a small amount of detergent; machine-dry on high heat and steam-press.

cut fabrics

Cut pieces in the following order. Patterns are on *page 151*.

To use freezer paper for cutting appliqué shapes, complete the following steps.

1. Lay freezer paper, shiny side down, over patterns. Use a pencil to trace each pattern once, leaving ½" between tracings. Cut out freezer-paper shapes roughly ¼" outside traced lines.

2. Using a hot dry iron, press freezer-paper shapes, shiny sides down, onto designated wools; let cool. Cut out wool shapes on drawn lines. Peel off freezer paper.

From brown wool, cut:
- 1 of Pattern A

From pink wool, cut:
- 1 each of patterns B and D

From white wool, cut:
- 1 of Pattern C

editor's tip

Sized perfectly to fit into the top of a parfait glass, this pincushion also is a clever cover-up for buttons, pins, and other small notions that can be stored in the base of the glass.

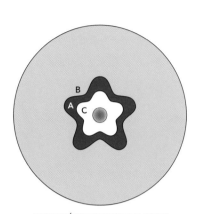

APPLIQUÉ PLACEMENT DIAGRAM

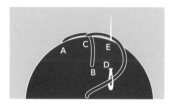

BLANKET STITCH DIAGRAM

appliqué and assemble pincushion

1. Referring to **Appliqué Placement Diagram**, center brown wool A piece on pink wool B circle; pin in place. Using two strands of brown embroidery floss, blanket-stitch brown piece in place.

   To blanket-stitch, pull needle up at A, form a reverse L shape with floss, and hold angle of L shape in place with your thumb (**Blanket Stitch Diagram**). Push needle down at B and come up at C to secure stitch. Continue in same manner.

2. Referring to **Appliqué Placement Diagram**, position white wool C piece on appliquéd circle; pin in place. Using two strands of brown embroidery floss, blanket-stitch white piece in place.

3. Sew red button to center of appliquéd circle to complete pincushion top.

4. Thread an embroidery needle with 36" of sewing thread; knot ends together. Work ⅛"-long gathering stitches about ¼" from edge of pincushion top. Pull up thread to gather slightly.

5. Place fiberfill in center of wrong side of pincushion top; pull gathers tight and secure thread.

(Turn pincushion top over to check firmness. If necessary, relax gathers and add more fiberfill before securing thread.)

6. Position pink wool D circle over gathered circle to cover gathering stitches.

7. Use one strand of pink sewing thread to whipstitch pincushion top and pink wool D circle together along edges to complete pincushion.

8. If desired, fill 4"-diameter parfait glass with white and pink buttons and top with pincushion.

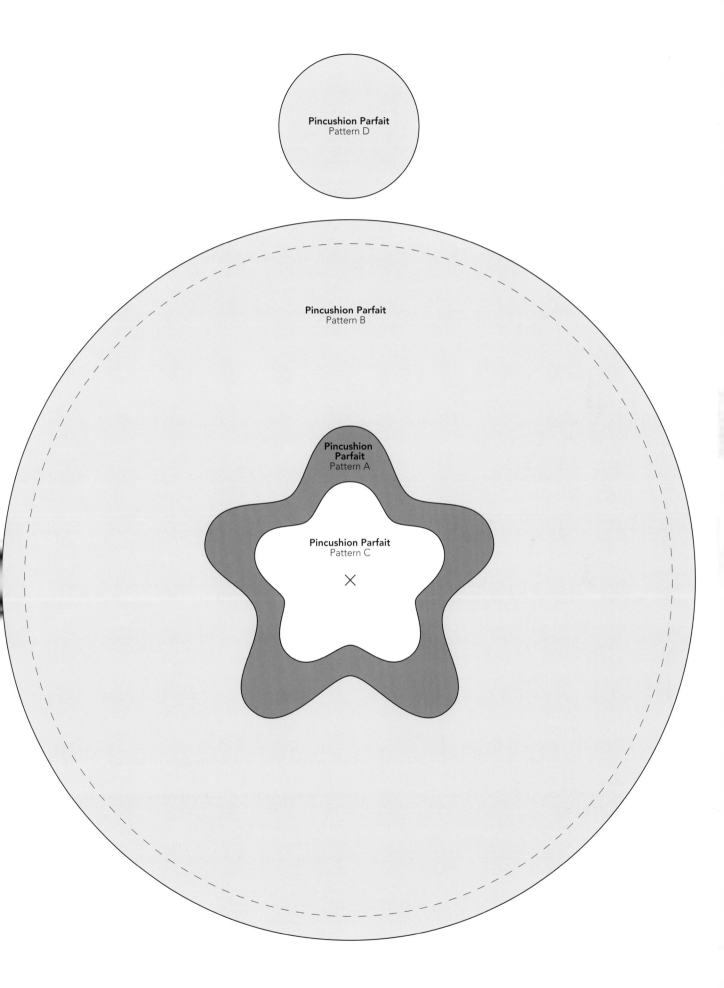

Pincushion Parfait
Pattern D

Pincushion Parfait
Pattern B

Pincushion
Parfait
Pattern A

Pincushion Parfait
Pattern C

You'll never guess what's hidden inside these petite pin holders. Underneath the layers of colorful felt, ribbon, and embellishments are plastic curlers that give the pincushions their cylindrical shape.

CHEAPER
by the dozen

DESIGNER **JEANNE PRYOR**
PHOTOGRAPHER **CAMERON SADEGHPOUR**

materials for one pincushion

- Scraps of yellow and white felt

- 1"-diameter, 1"-long plastic (magnetic) hair curler (to cut longer curlers to size, see Editor's Tip, *page 156*)

- Embroidery floss: yellow, white, bright pink, and orange

- 2—large-eye embroidery needles

- Polyester fiberfill

- 4½"-long piece novelty ribbon

- Cardboard

- Fabric glue

Finished pincushion: 1¼×2"

The following instructions make one pincushion, but you can have great fun using your own colorful combinations of felt, embroidery floss, ribbons, buttons, and mini accents to create delightful pincushions by the dozens.

cut fabrics

From yellow felt, cut:
- 1—1¼×4½" strip

From white felt, cut:
- 1—3"-diameter circle

assemble pincushion

1. Place open end of curler on cardboard and draw around circumference; cut out circle.

2. Repeat Step 1, drawing around circumference of curler on yellow felt; cut out circle.

3. Lay a thin line of glue around circumference of one side of cardboard circle. Stand curler on glue line and gently press in place. Allow to dry.

4. Wrap yellow felt 1¼×4½" strip around curler, lapping ends. Hold strip in place and, using a needle threaded with 40"-long, six-ply yellow floss, whipstitch lapped edge, working from top (open end) to bottom (cardboard-covered end). Do not cut thread.

editor's tip

When 1"-long curlers are not available, purchase longer curlers and cut to 1" lengths. To cut, mark curler in 1" segments. Place a coping saw securely in a vise with blade up. Rub curler back and forth over blade, rotating curler until segment is cut through. Rub cut edge of curler over sandpaper to smooth.

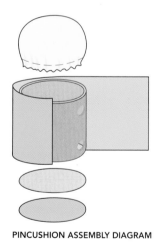

PINCUSHION ASSEMBLY DIAGRAM

5. Hold yellow felt circle in place over cardboard-covered end of curler and, starting at lapped end, whipstitch circle to bottom edge of felt-wrapped curler (**Pincushion Assembly Diagram**). Insert threaded needle under lapped edge and bring to top edge. Do not cut thread.

6. Using a second large-eye needle and six-ply white floss, sew a running stitch around circumference of white felt circle ¼" from outer edge (**Running Stitch Diagram** on *page 136*). Pull up thread to gather; pack tightly with polyester fiberfill and backstitch to make top. Clip thread.

7. Stitching side down, push top into base.

8. Pick up attached threaded needle and secure top to base with blanket stitches (**Blanket Stitch Diagram** on *page 136*, along with other stitches you can use for embellishing your pincushion). After last blanket stitch, push needle through top to opposite side, burying thread. Snip thread close to surface.

9. Use bright pink floss to sew a row of running stitches above blanket stitches and orange floss to sew below them.

10. Glue or stitch novelty ribbon to felt-wrapped curler to complete pincushion.

Inspired by a still-life portrait, this tomato, gourd, and carrot pincushion trio will look great sitting in a bowl by your sewing area.

DESIGNER **BARBARA CAMPBELL**
PHOTOGRAPHER **MARTY BALDWIN**

fruit &
veggies

materials for one *each* of carrot, gourd, and tomato pincushions

- 1—18×22" piece (fat quarter) *each* of orange floral, green floral, multicolor print, red dot

- Scrap of green print

- Lightweight fusible web

- Polyester fiberfill

- Zigzag-edge rotary cutter blade

- Needle and matching threads

Carrot pincushion: 14" long
Gourd pincushion: 5" tall
Tomato pincushion: 3½" tall

Quantities are for 100% cotton fabrics.
Measurements include ¼" seam allowances. Sew with right sides together unless otherwise stated.

cut fabrics for carrot pincushion

Instructions are given to make one pincushion.

Patterns are on *Pattern Sheet 1.* To make templates of patterns, see Make and Use Templates, *page 158.*

From orange floral, cut:
- 1 of Pattern A
From green floral, cut:
- 1—5×18" strip

assemble carrot pincushion

1. With right sides together, fold orange floral A piece in half lengthwise. Sew together long edges and short end at point. Turn right side out.

2. Firmly stuff with polyester fiberfill to make carrot. Hand-stitch with a long running stitch around the open end of the carrot, leaving long thread tails **(Diagram 1)**.

3. Using a decorative-edge blade in your rotary cutter, cut green floral 5×18" strip into ½"-wide strips, leaving 1" uncut at one end. Beginning at one end, roll up strip **(Diagram 2)** to make the carrot top.

4. Insert uncut end of carrot top into open end of the carrot. Pull thread tails to gather the carrot around the top. Hand-stitch the opening closed.

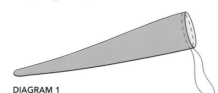

DIAGRAM 1

DIAGRAM 2

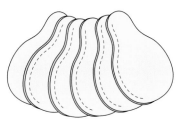

cut fabrics for gourd pincushion

Instructions are given to make one pincushion.

Patterns are on *Pattern Sheet 1*. To make templates of patterns, see Make and Use Templates, *page 158*.

From multicolor print, cut:
- 6 of Pattern B

From lightweight fusible web, cut:
- 1—1⅜×2¼" rectangle

assemble gourd pincushion

1. Sew together multicolor print B pieces in a row, leaving openings as indicated on the pattern piece (**Diagram 3**). Finger-press seams to one side.

2. Sew together ends to make a circle, leaving openings (**Diagram 4**) at the top and bottom. Stuff the gourd with polyester fiberfill but leave the top and bottom open.

3. Following the manufacturer's instructions, fuse fusible web 1⅜×2¼" rectangle to wrong side of green print scrap. Trim off excess green print. Fold fused rectangle in thirds lengthwise to make a 2¼"-long strip. Press with iron to make a stem.

4. Insert stem into top of pincushion and hand-sew the openings on the top and bottom of the pincushion closed, gathering the pieces at the side seams to create gourd shape.

cut fabrics for tomato pincushion

Instructions are given to make one pincushion.

Patterns are on *Pattern Sheet 1*. To make templates of patterns, see Make and Use Templates, *page 158*.

From red dot, cut:
- 6 of Pattern C

From lightweight fusible web, trace:
- 2 of Pattern D. Cut out roughly ¼" around traced lines.

assemble tomato pincushion

1. Sew together red dot C pieces in a row (**Diagram 5**). Finger-press seams to one side.

2. Sew together ends to make the tomato, leaving an opening in the bottom for stuffing (**Diagram 6**).

3. Firmly stuff the tomato with polyester fiberfill. Hand-sew the bottom opening closed, tucking in raw edges.

4. Following the manufacturer's instructions, fuse one fusible web E leaf onto wrong side of a green floral scrap. Cut out leaf on drawn line. Fuse leaf to wrong side of another green floral scrap. Trim off excess to complete a leaf. Repeat to make a second leaf.

5. Hand-stitch leaves to top of tomato.

DIAGRAM 3

DIAGRAM 4

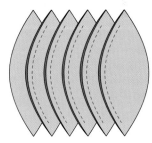

DIAGRAM 5

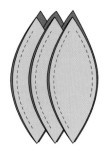

DIAGRAM 6

back to basics

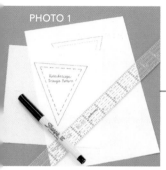
PHOTO 1

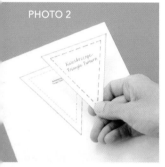
PHOTO 2

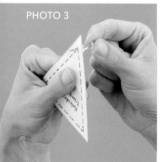
PHOTO 3

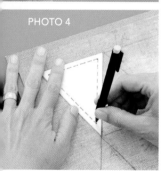
PHOTO 4

PHOTO 5

make and use templates

When making templates, use easy-to-cut transparent template plastic, available at crafts supply stores.

To make a template, lay the plastic over a printed pattern. Trace the pattern using a permanent marker (and ruler for straight lines). Mark template with project name, letter, and any marked matching points (**Photo 1**).

For machine piecing, the solid lines are cutting lines, and dashed lines are seam lines. (An arrow on a pattern indicates the direction the fabric grain should run.)

Cut out the template and check it against the original pattern for accuracy (**Photo 2**). Any error (even if small) will multiply as you assemble the project.

Using a pushpin, make a hole in the template at all marked matching points (**Photo 3**). The hole must be large enough to accommodate a pencil point.

To trace the template on fabric, use a pencil, a dressmaker's white pencil, chalk, or a special fabric marker that makes a thin, accurate line. Don't use a ballpoint or ink pen, which may bleed. Test all marking tools on a fabric scrap before using them. Place your fabric right side down on 220-grit sandpaper to prevent the fabric from stretching as you trace. Place the template facedown on the wrong side of the fabric with the template's grain line parallel to the fabric's lengthwise or crosswise grain. Trace around the template. Mark any matching points through the holes in the template (**Photo 4**). (When sewing pieces together, line up and pin through matching points to ensure accurate assembly.)

Repeat to trace the number of pieces needed, positioning the tracings without space between them. Use shears or scissors (or a rotary cutter and ruler) to precisely cut fabric pieces on the drawn lines (**Photo 5**).

For appliqué and hand piecing, the dashed lines indicate finished size; add needed seam allowance as instructed in project.

piece and appliqué

stitching: Quilting depends upon accuracy at every step. Use exact ¼" seam allowances throughout a quilt's construction. It isn't necessary to backstitch at the beginning of any seam that will be intersected by another seam later in the quiltmaking process. Use a stitch length of 10–12 stitches per inch (2.0- to 2.5-mm setting) to prevent stitches from unraveling before they're stitched over again. Secure seams that won't be sewn across again (such as those in borders) with a few backstitches.

pinning: When you want seams to line up perfectly, match up seams of pieced units, and then place an extra-fine pin diagonally through the pieces, catching both seam allowances. Avoid sewing over pins because this can damage your machine and injure you.

pressing: Pressing seams ensures accurate piecing. Set the seam first by pressing it as it was sewn, without opening the fabric pieces. This helps sink the stitches into the fabric, leaving you with a less bulky seam allowance.

The direction you press the seam allowance is important and is usually specified in the instructions. Typically you will press the entire seam to one side rather than open. When two seams will be joined, press the seams in opposite directions; this helps line up the seams perfectly and reduces bulk.

Make sure you are pressing, not ironing. Ironing means moving the iron while it is in contact with the fabric; this stretches and distorts seams. Pressing involves lifting the iron off the surface of the fabric and putting it back down in another location.

machine appliqué: Many fast-and-easy appliqué projects are meant to be fused, then secured with stitching. Follow the directions in the project instructions for how to prepare appliqué pieces for fusing.

Precise ¼" seams allow you to join units, blocks, and rows with ease.

Pivoting outside curves. When appliquéing, position the presser foot so the left swing of the needle lands on the appliqué and the right swing of the needle lands just on the foundation, grazing the appliqué (**Photo 6**).

Stop at the first pivot point with the needle down in the fabric on the right-hand swing of the needle (see first red dot in **Diagram 1;** the arrow indicates the stitching direction). Raise the presser foot, pivot the fabric slightly, and stitch to the next pivot point. Repeat as needed to round the entire outer curve.

To help you know when to pivot, mark the edges of circular or oval appliqué pieces with the hours of a clock; pivot the fabric at each mark (**Photo 7**).

Turning outside corners. When turning a corner, knowing where to stop and pivot makes a big difference in the finished look of your appliqué stitches.

Stop with the needle down in the fabric on the right-hand swing of the needle (see red dot in **Diagram 2**). Raise the presser foot and pivot the fabric. Lower the presser foot and begin stitching the next edge (**Diagram 3**).

hand appliqué: To make a project portable, substitute hand appliqué for fusible appliqué. Add a ³⁄₁₆" seam allowance to pattern pieces when cutting them out; press seam allowances under. Tack-stitch appliqués to foundation using a sharp, between, straw, or milliner's needle and the finest thread you can find that matches the appliqué pieces.

Slip-stitch the edges. Pin or baste the appliqué to the appliqué foundation. Thread a hand-sewing needle with 18" of thread.

Slip-stitch the appliqué edge in place by passing the needle up through the foundation and folded edge of the appliqué and then back through the appliqué foundation (**Photo 8**). Continue around the appliqué, taking smaller stitches around inside corners and curves.

Finish it. End by knotting the thread on the wrong side of the foundation, beneath the appliqué piece. Once all pieces have been appliquéd, place the foundation facedown on a terry cloth towel and press from the wrong side to prevent flattening the appliqués.

cutting on the bias

Bias runs diagonally between the lengthwise and crosswise grain lines of a woven fabric. The true bias runs exactly at a 45° angle to the grain lines (**Diagram 4,** *page 160*) and has the most stretch in a woven fabric.

Because of their built-in stretch, strips cut on the bias can be easily curved or shaped. Use them when binding curved edges or to make curved appliqué pieces such as vines or stems.

You can also cut directional fabrics such as plaids or stripes on the bias for purely visual reasons. A bias binding cut from a striped fabric creates a "barber pole" effect.

cutting bias strips: To cut bias strips, begin with a fabric square or rectangle. Using an acrylic ruler and a rotary cutter, cut one edge at a 45° angle. Measure the desired width from the cut edge and then make a cut parallel to the edge (**Photo 9**). Repeat until you have the desired number of strips. Handle bias strips carefully to avoid distorting the fabric.

PHOTO 6

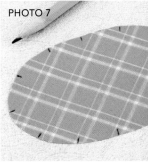

PHOTO 7

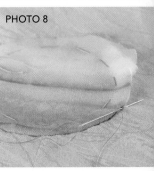

PHOTO 8

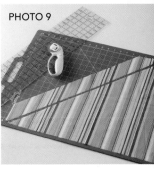

PHOTO 9

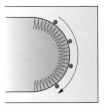

DIAGRAM 1

DIAGRAM 2

DIAGRAM 3

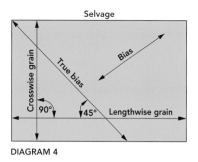

Selvage

Crosswise grain

True bias

Bias

90°   45°   Lengthwise grain

DIAGRAM 4

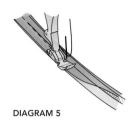

DIAGRAM 5

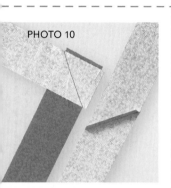

PHOTO 10

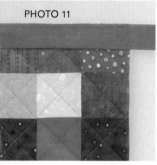

PHOTO 11

PHOTO 12

PHOTO 13

covered cording

Covered cording is made by sewing a bias-cut fabric strip around a length of cording. The width of the bias strip will vary depending on the diameter of your cording. Refer to the specific project instructions for those measurements. Regardless, the method used to cover the cording is the same.

With the wrong side inside, fold under 1½" at one end of the bias strip. With wrong side inside, fold the strip in half lengthwise to make the cording cover. Insert the cording next to the folded edge, placing a cording end 1" from the cording cover folded end. Using a machine cording foot, sew through both fabric layers right next to the cording (Diagram 5).

When attaching the cording to your project, begin stitching 1½" from the covered cording's folded end.

After going around the entire edge of the project, cut the end of the cording so that it will fit snugly into the folded opening at the beginning. The ends of the cording should abut inside the covering. Stitch the ends in place to secure.

complete the quilt

assemble the layers: Cut and piece the backing fabric to measure at least 3" bigger than the quilt top on all sides. Press seams open. Place the quilt backing wrong side up on a flat surface. Center and smooth the batting atop the quilt backing. Center the quilt top right side up on top of the batting and smooth out any wrinkles. Use safety pins or long hand stitches to baste the layers together.

quilt as desired: A few of the more common machine-quilting methods follow.

Stitching in the ditch. Stitch just inside a seam line; the stitches should almost disappear into the seam. Using a walking foot attachment on your sewing machine will help prevent the quilt layers from shifting.

Stipple quilting. This random, allover stitching provides texture and interest behind a pattern. Use a darning foot and lower the feed dogs on your machine.

Outline quilting. Stitch ¼" from a seam line or the edge of an appliqué shape, just past the extra thickness of the seam allowance.

trim quilt: Trim the batting and backing fabric even with the quilt top edges; machine-baste a scant ¼" from quilt top edges if desired. (Some quilters prefer to wait until they have machine-sewn the binding to the quilt top before trimming the batting and backing.)

better binding

cut the strips: The cutting instructions for each project tell you the width and number of binding strips to cut. Unless otherwise specified, cut binding strips on the straight grain of the fabric. Join the binding strips with diagonal seams to make one long binding strip (Photo 10). Trim seams to ¼" and press open.

attach the binding: With the wrong side inside, fold under 1" at one end of the binding strip and press. Then fold the strip in half lengthwise with the wrong side inside. Place the binding strip against the right side of the quilt top along one edge, aligning the binding strip's raw edges with the quilt top's raw edge (do not start at a corner). Begin sewing the binding in place 2" from the folded end.

turn the corner: Stop sewing when you're ¼" from the corner (or a distance equal to the seam allowance you're using). Backstitch; then clip the threads (Photo 11). Remove the quilt from under the sewing-machine presser foot.

Fold the binding strip upward, creating a diagonal fold, and finger-press (Photo 12).

Holding the diagonal fold in place with your finger, bring the binding strip down in line with the next edge, making a horizontal fold that aligns with the quilt edge. Start sewing again at the top of the horizontal fold, stitching through all layers (Photo 13). Sew around the quilt, turning each corner in the same manner.

finish it: When you return to the starting point, encase the binding strip's raw edge inside the folded end and finish sewing to the starting point. Trim the batting and backing fabric even with the quilt top edges if not done earlier.

Turn the binding over the edge to the back. Hand-stitch the binding to the backing fabric only, covering any machine stitching. To make the binding corners on the quilt back match the mitered corners on the quilt front, hand-stitch up to a corner and make a fold in the binding. Secure the fold with a couple stitches; then continue stitching the binding in place along the next edge.